Collector's Digest
Flashlights
PRICE GUIDE

1995 Values

By L-W Book Sales

© 1995

L-W Book Sales
P.O Box 69
Gas City, IN. 46933

ISBN#: 0-89538-033-1

Copyright 1995 By L-W Books.

All rights reserved. No part of this work may be reproduced or used in any forms or by any means - graphic, electronic, or mechanical, including photocopying or storage and retrieval systems - without written permission from the copyright holder.

Published by: L-W Book Sales
                  P.O. Box 69
                  Gas City IN. 46933

Please write for our free catalog.

Attention Collectors . . . if you would like to contribute photographs or information of your collection (possibly for profit), please call L-W Books (toll free) at 1-800-777-6450 Tuesday thru Friday 9am to 3pm.

TABLE OF CONTENTS

Title Page. 1

Copyright Page. 2

Table of Contents. 3

Introduction. 4

Acknowledgments 5

Catalog Pages. 6-42

Flashlight Photographs A-Z. 43-86

Advertising & Displays. 87-97

Character Lights. 98-111

Pen-Lights. 112-116

Novelty Lights. 117-126

Lanterns. 127-142

INTRODUCTION

Since the late nineteenth century when Thomas Alva Edison generously offered his gift of artificial light to the modern world, Americans have adapted this concept to every facet of life. Lights had soon been conformed for specific or practical uses such as reading lamps, headlamps on motor vehicles, business signs, and even lights designed for use underwater. The dawn of the twentieth century, however, provided one of the most utilitarian devices to utilize the electric light technology - the portable flashlight.

Due to the introduction of the flashlight, modern men's work habits were forever changed. Safer than a lantern and not as heavy, the flashlight made all night-time tasks much simpler. No longer would an avid explorer be lost in the dark of the woods, nor shall coal miners complain from the stench or awkwardness of the ol' bullseye lantern. Today the flashlight remains a staple tool for just about every homemaker, farmer, and blue collar worker. While the more contemporary models of flashlights contrast slightly with the older ones, the old flashlights are worth more in historical value and monetary value as well, as collectors have taken to flashlights as have moths to the flame.

Veteran flashlights may be discovered with many opportunities. Antique mall shops and dealers may yield some worthwhile finds, yet the best opportunity may rest in the collectible tool field. Antique tool shows and collector's booths should present a decent selection of aged flashlights, both by popular manufacturers and lesser-known companies. Collectors' newletters and ad papers may include classifieds or sales ads offering flashlights, and "want" ads from other flashlight collectors may offer clues as to sources to gather information and new pieces for your own collection.

While making your flashlight aquisitions, there are a few helpful hints as to making an estimation of any certain flashlight's age. One good way to determine age is examining the switch operation and the lens shape. Most early flashlights (1900-1910's) had external switch operations, where the two metal contacts were affixed to the outside wall of the flashlight frame. The lens shape is instrumental to identifying older flashlights as well. The convex shape of the bullseye lens should indicate an early specimen, as these were produced up until the flat-faced lens was introduced in the 1930's.

While exploring the realms of collectible flashlights, you may prepare yourself for the search of new additions to your collection. Maintain a sense of discretion, carry some extra batteries, and bring along a copy of *Flashlights - A Price Guide* to shed some light on the subject!

ACKNOWLEDGMENTS & PRICING INFO

On behalf of L-W Books we would like to thank the following people: Don Perkins of Indianapolis, IN.
    Denton Howard of Jonesboro, IN.
    Howard Johnson of Marion, IN.
    Al Wilson of Las Vegas, NV.
    Wayne Stoops of Ft. Wayne, IN.
    Jim & Erin Richards of Gas City, IN.
    Old Tyme Toy Mall of Fairmount, IN.
    Phil Atkinson of Mercer, PA.

The value of a flashlight or electric lantern may fluctuate depending on condition. Dented walls or cracked lenses will lower prices while flashlights in the original box or display will elevate prices. Also, any type of cartoon or figural flashlight with special features (Whistles, Sirens or Multi-Colored Lenses) may attain a handsome price.

Even though this is a reference guide for collecting flashlights, L-W Books will not be held responsible for profits or losses incurred as a result of consulting this guide.

Catalog & Magazine Ads

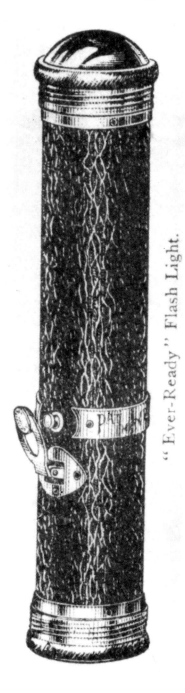

Original 1902 Catalog Page.

FLASH AND SEARCH LIGHTS

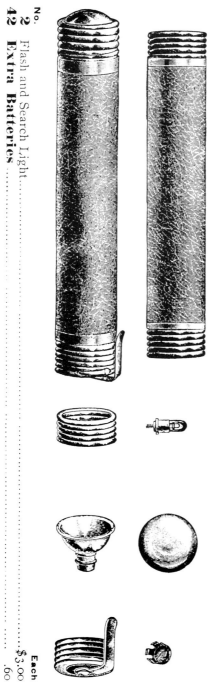

Original 1904 Catalog Page.

No.		Each
2	Flash and Search Light	$3.00
42	**Extra Batteries**	.60

Size, 1½ x 9 inches. Gives from 8,000 to 10,000 flashes, 7 to 8 hours continuous use. Battery good for three months. Press switch for Flash Light. For Search or Continuous Light turn switch to right until it comes in contact with the raised connection on switch cap. Battery can be taken out or put in at either end.

Eveready Miners' Flash Light

Large lens and reflector. Spreads and intensifies the light in a manner that better adapts it for many purposes. Can be used by miners to advantage for exploring underground passages, and satisfactorily meets the requirements of camp life.

The lens is of large diameter and the light is provided with a powerful reflector.

No. 2616. Diameter 1½ in; length 6½ in; 2½-volt lamp complete with Tungsten battery and Mazda bulb, in a vulcanized fibre case.
Weight, ¾ lb. $1.60
Renewal Tungsten Battery No. 790.
Weight, ½ lb. $0.25

Eveready Tubular Flash Light

A convenient and compact light, used by those who work at night or are obliged to visit dark places at home or abroad. Great care is taken in the manufacture of these lights and they are high grade in every sense of the word, all material and workmanship undergoing a rigid inspection.

Since their introduction they have saved millions of dollars in fire loss. Danger from fire is eliminated, as matches are not required for lighting them. May be used with freedom around leaking gas, oil, powder or other combustibles. Should be in every home, store, office and factory.

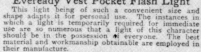

No. 2612. Diameter 1½ in.; length 8½ in.; 3½-volt lamp. Complete with Tungsten battery and Mazda bulb, in a vulcanized fibre case. Weight, 1 lb. $1.60
Renewal Tungsten Battery No. 705. Weight, ¼ lb. .... $ .30

Eveready Electric House Lamp

For use around the house, in the yard and out-houses, down in the cellar and in closets full of clothes. The lamps can be brushed against the most inflammable fabrics, stood beside a kerosene oil can, even set on the stove, and no harm can result. Equipped with the new Tungsten battery, this is an indispensible type of house lamp.

Cases are in polished oak and ebony; the trimmings are polished nickel. The lamps are light and clean and illuminate in a brilliant manner. Has 3-cell battery and 3½-volt lamp.
No. 4703. Weight, 1½ lbs. Complete.. $2.25
Renewal Tungsten Battery No. 734. Weight, 1 lb. .... .35

Eveready Vest Pocket Flash Light

This light being of such a convenient size and shape adapts it for personal use. The instances in which a light is temporarily required for immediate use are so numerous that a light of this character should be in the possession of everyone. The best material and workmanship obtainable are employed in their manufacture.

No. 6951. 1 x1⅞x3½ in., 2½-volt lamp. Complete with Tungsten battery and Mazda bulb in a black celluloid case. Weight, 4 oz. ..$1.20
Renewal Tungsten Battery No. 792. Weight, 2 oz. $0.25
No. 6909. 1x2¾x3½ inches; 3½-volt lamp. Complete with Tungsten battery and Mazda bulb in a vulcanized fibre case. Weight, 8 oz. $1.25
Renewal Tungsten Battery No. 703. Weight, 6 oz. $0.30

Eveready Miniature Vest Pocket Light

Case made of brass, heavily nickel plated and polished. Contact buttons made to represent jewels. Equipped with Tungsten battery and Mazda bulb.
No. 6961. 2⅞x1⅜x¾ inches; 2½ volt lamp. Weight, 3 oz. $1.00
Renewal Tungsten Battery No. 750. Weight, 2 oz. $0.25

Eveready Watchman's Lantern

As this is the most serviceable type of lantern made for outdoor work, it seems certain to supplant those now used by signalmen, conductors, trackmen, brakemen, switchmen, etc. Turned on and off instantly as required without the use of matches. Wind and storm have no effect upon its service.

The lantern has an extra large lens and reflector and throws a wide circle of light. Being electric, all danger from fire or explosion is eliminated, and it may be handled with entire safety wherever inflammable material or explosives are exposed. No wick to trim and no oil to spill. The lanterns are highly polished nickel finish throughout.
No. 4701. Weight, 2½ lbs. Complete $3.75
Renewal Tungsten Battery No. 710. Weight, 1¼ lbs. .... .60

Electric Bells and Buzzer Class "A"

Class A bells and buzzers have cast iron covers and base with nickel plated gong. Every detail of the bell and buzzer is constructed so as to give durable and satisfactory service. Can be adjusted.
2½ in. gong, 6 oz. $0.30
4 in. gong, 12 oz. .... .38
Buzzer, 4 oz. .... .30
Operated on one cell of battery.

Original 1914 Catalog Page.

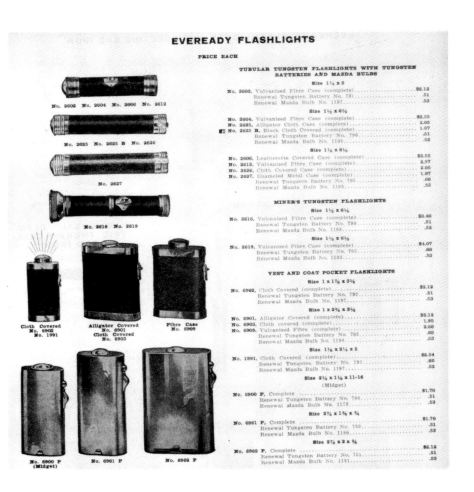

Original 1915 Catalog Page.

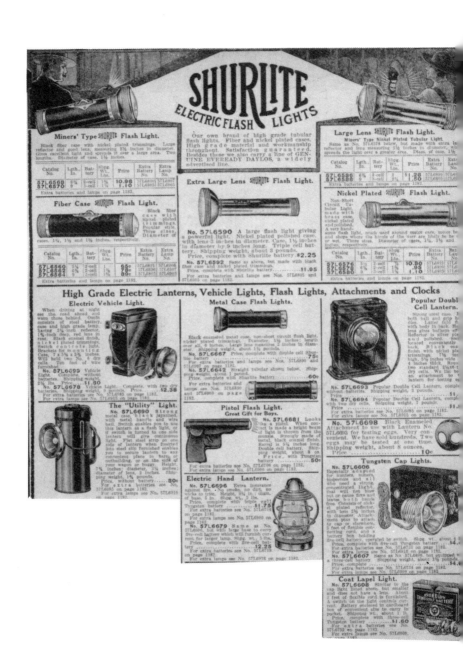

Original 1918 Catalog Page.

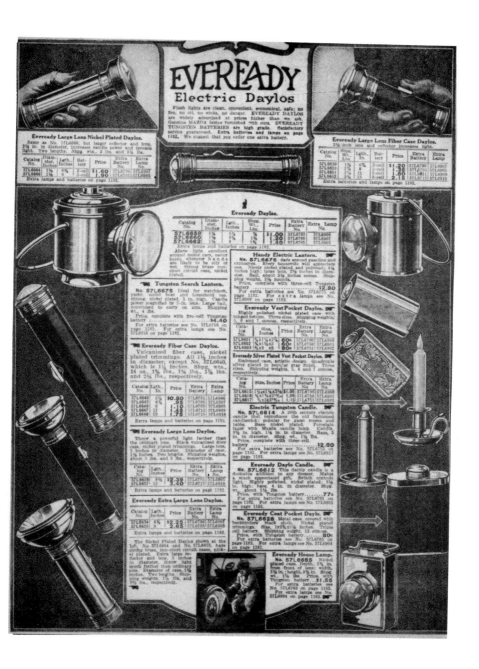

Original 1918 Catalog Page.

Original 1919 Catalog Page.

Flashlights, Batteries and Bulbs (Continued)

THE FRANCO WAY
"Wire Concealed"
imbedded in fibre

THE OLD WAY
"Wire Exposed"
to corrosion and breakage

Tubular Fibre Flashlights "Wire Concealed"

4687
2-Cell Baby Tubular, size 1¼x5 inches.
Price per doz. cases and lamps..........$6.25
Price per doz., complete..................$8.10
Price each, complete.......................70c.

4688
2-Cell Regular Tubular, size 1½x6½ inches.
Price per doz. cases and lamps..........$8.10
Price per doz., complete.................$10.30
Price each, complete.......................88c.

4689
3-Cell Regular Tubular, size 1½x8¼ inches.
Price per doz. cases and lamps..........$9.00
Price per doz., complete.................$12.00
Price each, complete.......................$1.05

3518
2-Cell Baby Miner's Reflector, size 1¼x6¼ inches.
Price per doz. cases and lamps..........$7.20
Price per doz., complete..................$8.50
Price each, complete.......................75c.

3394
2-Cell Penlite, nickel finish.
Price per doz. cases and lamps..........$4.10
Price per doz., complete..................$5.75
Price each, complete.......................50c.

4690
2-Cell Miner's Reflector, size 1¼x6½ inches.
Price per doz. cases and lamps.........$10.00
Price per doz., complete.................$12.00
Price each, complete.......................$1.05

4691
3-Cell Miner's Reflector, size 1½x8½ inches.
Price per doz. cases and lamps.........$10.60
Price per doz., complete.................$13.50
Price each, complete.......................$1.15

4449
2-Cell Searchlight Reflector, size 1¼x6½ inches.
Price per doz. cases and lamps.........$14.50
Price per doz., complete.................$16.70
Price each, complete.......................$1.45

2-Cell Pistol Light, Black Enamel.

4755
Price per doz. cases and lamps.$8.70
Price per doz., complete....$10.50
Price each, complete........90c.

Original 1919 Catalog Page.

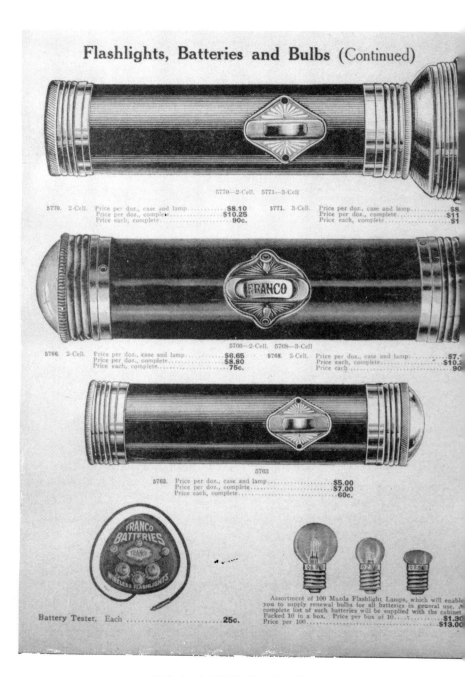

Original 1919 Catalog Page.

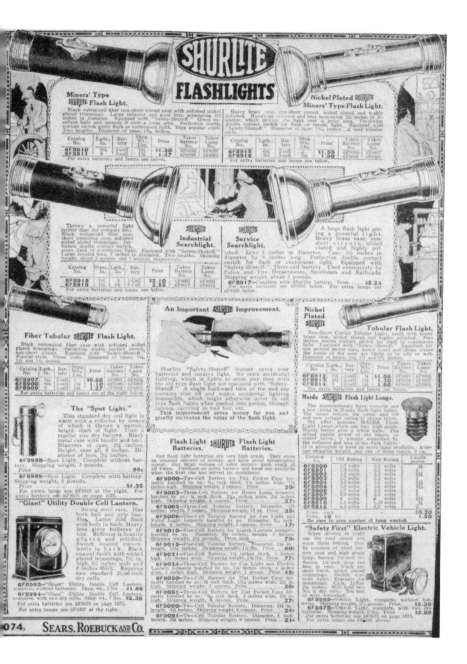

Original 1921 Catalog Page.

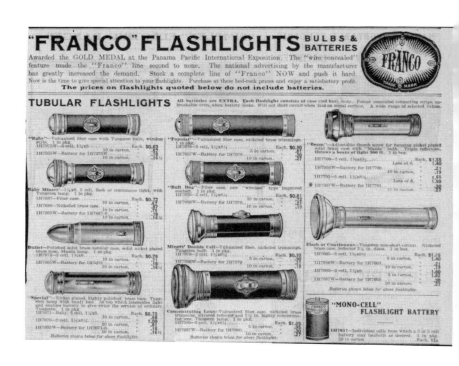

Original 1921 Catalog Page.

The fall rush for Eveready Flashlights and Batteries is beginning and will increase rapidly from now on—the result of the shorter days and longer evenings

The demand for Eveready Flashlight Batteries is long established—constant month after month, year in and year out. They fit and improve all makes of flashlights; they give a brighter light; *they last longer.* Only two sizes to stock—little investment, easy sales, faster turnover, greater profits.

It'll pay you to concentrate on Eveready Flashlights and Batteries now—and push hard!

Write Your Jobber Today

NATIONAL CARBON COMPANY, Inc.
Long Island City, N. Y.

Atlanta   Chicago   Cleveland   Kansas City   San Francisco

Please Mention "The Dealer."

EVEREADY STANDARD TUBULAR FLASHLIGHT FOR INDOOR USE

It takes but a small investment to carry a well assorted stock of Eveready Flashlights

Original 1922 Catalog Page.

Original 1925 Catalog Page.

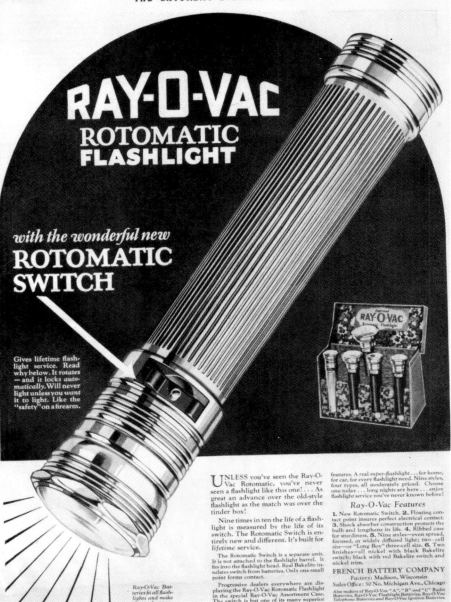

Original 1928 Catalog Page.

YALE FLASHLIGHTS

Any flashlight, whether it be a two or three cell, nickel, or fibre, regular, miner, searchlight or spot-light type, may be converted into a candle light by removing the complete head assembly and standing the light on end. Equipped with selective type switch that will give a flash contact or permanent contact as desired. Bulb is inserted in a groove at open end of hood permitting bulb to slip into perfect alignment through opening of reflector base; fitted with shock absorber to protect bulb against accidental jolts. Small brass collar insures perfect contact at all times. End cap has flat strip of phosphor spring bronze with raised center. Lens rings are all octagon shaped with smooth slightly rounded edges; stays where it is put. Lens made from finest quality French plate glass. Head-hood reflector lens and lens ring are combined into a single unit, assuring absolutely perfect alignment. The reflector surface is never touched by hands when replacing bulb, entirely dustproof always preserving clean, smooth surface of reflector and inner side of lens. Complete with bulbs less batteries.

REGULAR TYPE, TWO CELL

Size 5⅝x1⅜ in. With bulb only, less batteries.

No. 2001 Flashlight. Fibre case ..each, **$1.35**
No. 2002 Flashlight. Nickel case each, **1.70**

One in a carton

Requires 2 No. 101 Mono-Cells .. each, $0.15-
Renewal Mazda Lamp No. 11, 2.2 volts .... each, .12-

REGULAR TYPE, TWO CELL

Size 6¼x1⅜ in. With bulb only, less batteries.

No. 2101 Flashlight. Fibre case. .each, **$1.35**

One in a carton

Requires 2 No. 102 Mono-Cells ..each, $0.15-
Renewal Mazda Lamp No. 16, 2.4 volts .... each, .12-

REGULAR TYPE, THREE CELL

Size 9⅛x1⅜ in. With bulb only, less batteries.

No. 3101 Flashlight. Fibre case. ..each, **$2.00**

One in a carton

Requires 3 No. 102 Mono-Cells ..each, $0.15-
Renewal Mazda Lamp No. 17, 3.6 volts .... each, .12-

MINERS' TYPE, TWO CELL

Size 6x1¾ in. With bulb only, less batteries.

No. 2003 Flashlight. Fibre case ..each, **$1.70**

One in a carton

Requires 2 No. 101 Mono-Cells ..each, $0.15-
Renewal Mazda Lamp No. 11, 2.33 volts .... each, .12-

MINERS' TYPE, TWO CELL

Size 6⅝x2½ in. With bulb only, less batteries.

No. 2103 Flashlight. Fibre case ..each, **$1.70**

One in a carton

Requires 2 No. 102 Mono-Cells ..each, $0.15-
Renewal Mazda Lamp No. 16, 2.4 volts .... each, .12-

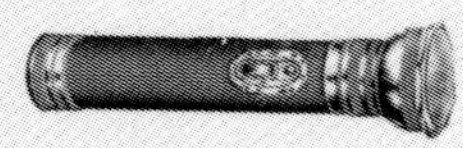

MINERS' TYPE, THREE CELL

Size 9¼x2½ in. With bulb only, less batteries.

No. 3103 Flashlight. Fibre case ..each, **$2.55**

One in a carton

Requires 3 No. 102 Mono-Cells each, $0.15-
Renewal Mazda Lamp No. 17, 3.6 volts .... each, .12-

TWO CELL SPOTLIGHT

Size 6¼x2⅛ in. With concentrated bulb, less batteries.

No. 2201 Spotlight. Fibre case each, **$1.70**

One in a carton

Requires 2 No. 102 Mono-Cells ..each, $0.15-
Renewal Mazda Lamp No. 14, 2.4 volts .... each, .15-

THREE CELL SPOTLIGHT

Size 8[illegible]2⅛ in. With concentrated bulb, less batteries.

No. 3201 Spotlight. Fibre case ...each, **$1.70**

One in a carton

Requires 3 No. 102 Mono-Cells each, $0.15-
Renewal Mazda Lamp No. 13, 3.6 volts .... each, .15-

FOCUSING THREE CELL SEARCHLIGHT

Size 9¼x3⅜ in. With concentrated bulb, less batteries.

No. 3205 Searchlight. Fibre case each, **$4.70**

One in a carton

Requires 3 No. 102 Mono-Cells each, $0.15-
Renewal Mazda Lamp No. 13, 3.6 volts .... each, .15-

FOCUSING FIVE CELL SEARCHLIGHT

Size 14⅞x3⅜ in. With concentrated bulb, less batteries.

No. 5206 Searchlight. Nickel case each, **$7.00**

One in a carton

Requires 5 No. 102 Mono-Cells each, $0.15-
Renewal Mazda Lamp No. 31, 6.2 volts .... each, .15-

TRI-COLOR, THREE BULB FLASHLIGHT

Size 9⅝x3¾ in. With three bulbs, all clear, or one each clear, red and green, less batteries.

No. 3401 Flashlight. Fibre case. .each, **$5.40**

One in a carton

Requires 3 No. 102 Mono-Cells ..each, $0.15-
Clear renewal Mazda lamps, No. 17, 3.6 volts .... each, .15-
Colored renewal Mazda Lamps, No. 17, 3.6 volts .... each, .18-

HANDI-LITE, TWO CELL

A flashlight with collapsible stand which can be set in any position directing the light wherever desired. Nickel plated. Complete with Mono-Cells.

No. 2510 Handi-Lite .... each, **$1.70**

One in a carton

Requires 2 No. 102 Mono-Cells ..each, $0.15-
Renewal Mazda Lamps No. 16, 2.4 volt .... each, .12-

Original 1928 Catalog Page.

Original 1928 Catalog Page.

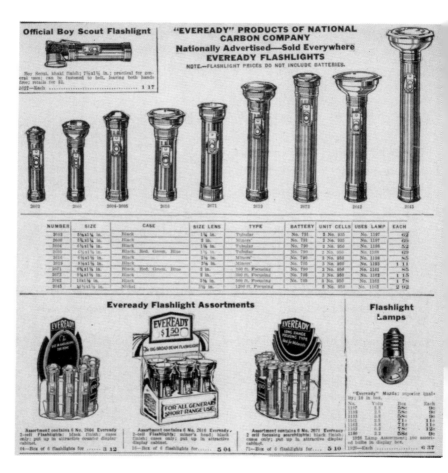

Original 1930 Catalog Page.

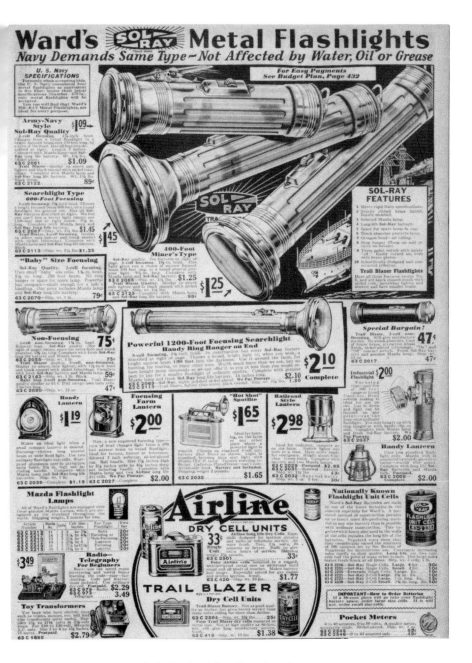

Original 1931 Catalog Page.

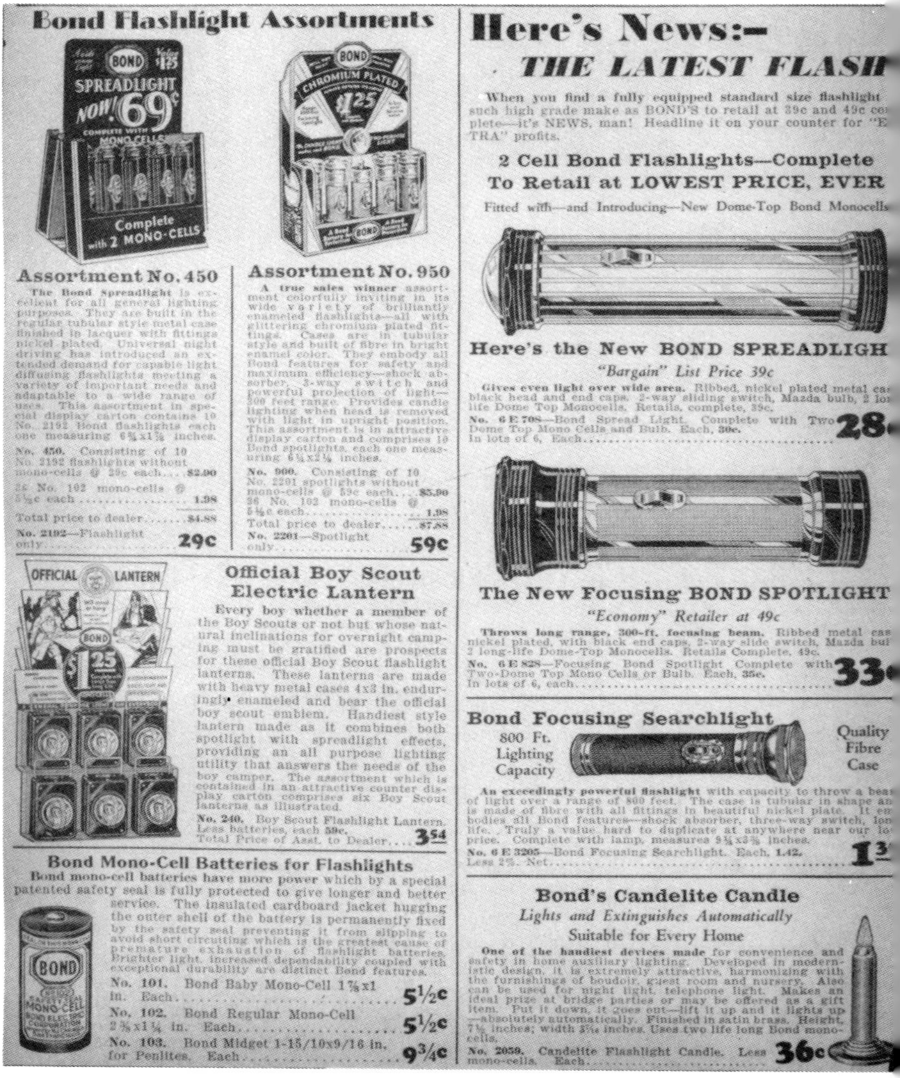

Bond Flashlight Assortments

Assortment No. 450

The Bond Spreadlight is excellent for all general lighting purposes. They are built in the regular tubular style metal case finished in lacquer with fittings nickel plated. Universal night driving has introduced an extended demand for capable light diffusing flashlights meeting a variety of important needs and adaptable to a wide range of uses. This assortment in special display carton contains 10 No. 2192 Bond flashlights each one measuring 6⅝x1½ inches.

No. 450. Consisting of 10 No. 2192 flashlights without mono-cells @ 29c each.... $2.90
36 No. 102 mono-cells @ 5½c each.... 1.98
Total price to dealer.... $4.88
No. 2192—Flashlight only.... **29c**

Assortment No. 950

A true sales winner assortment colorfully inviting in its wide variety of brilliantly enameled flashlights—all with glittering chromium plated fittings. Cases are in tubular style and built of fibre in bright enamel color. They embody all Bond features for safety and maximum efficiency—shock absorber, 3-way switch and powerful projection of light—300 feet range. Provides candle lighting when head is removed with light in upright position. This assortment is in attractive display carton and comprises 10 Bond spotlights, each one measuring 6⅛x2⅛ inches.

No. 950. Consisting of 10 No. 2201 spotlights without mono-cells @ 59c each.... $5.90
36 No. 102 mono-cells @ 5½c each.... 1.98
Total price to dealer.... $7.88
No. 2201—Spotlight only.... **59c**

Official Boy Scout Electric Lantern

Every boy whether a member of the Boy Scouts or not but whose natural inclinations for overnight camping must be gratified are prospects for these official Boy Scout flashlight lanterns. These lanterns are made with heavy metal cases 4x3 in. enduringly enameled and bear the official boy scout emblem. Handiest style lantern made as it combines both spotlight with spreadlight effects, providing an all purpose lighting utility that answers the needs of the boy camper. The assortment which is contained in an attractive counter display carton comprises six Boy Scout lanterns as illustrated.

No. 240. Boy Scout Flashlight Lantern. Less batteries, each 59c.
Total Price of Asst. to Dealer.... **3.54**

Bond Mono-Cell Batteries for Flashlights

Bond mono-cell batteries have more power which by a special patented safety seal is fully protected to give longer and better service. The insulated cardboard jacket hugging the outer shell of the battery is permanently fixed by the safety seal preventing it from slipping to avoid short circuiting which is the greatest cause of premature exhaustion of flashlight batteries. Brighter light, increased dependability coupled with exceptional durability are distinct Bond features.

No. 101. Bond Baby Mono-Cell 1⅞x1 in. Each.... **5½c**
No. 102. Bond Regular Mono-Cell 2⅜x1¼ in. Each.... **5½c**
No. 103. Bond Midget 1-15/16x9/16 in. for Penlites. Each.... **9¾c**

Here's News:—
THE LATEST FLASH

When you find a fully equipped standard size flashlight such high grade make as BOND'S to retail at 39c and 49c co[m]plete—it's NEWS, man! Headline it on your counter for "E[X]TRA" profits.

2 Cell Bond Flashlights—Complete To Retail at LOWEST PRICE, EVER

Fitted with—and Introducing—New Dome-Top Bond Monocells

Here's the New BOND SPREADLIGH[T]

"Bargain" List Price 39c

Gives even light over wide area. Ribbed, nickel plated metal ca[se], black head and end caps. 2-way sliding switch, Mazda bulb, 2 lo[ng] life Dome Top Monocells. Retails, complete, 39c.

No. 6 E 708—Bond Spread Light. Complete with Two Dome Top Mono Cells and Bulb. Each, 30c.
In lots of 6, Each.... **28**

The New Focusing BOND SPOTLIGHT

"Economy" Retailer at 49c

Throws long range, 300-ft. focusing beam. Ribbed metal cas[e], nickel plated, with black end caps, 2-way slide switch, Mazda bu[lb], 2 long-life Dome-Top Monocells. Retails Complete, 49c.

No. 6 E 828—Focusing Bond Spotlight Complete with Two-Dome Top Mono Cells or Bulb. Each, 35c.
In lots of 6, each.... **33**

Bond Focusing Searchlight

800 Ft. Lighting Capacity

Quality Fibre Case

An exceedingly powerful flashlight with capacity to throw a bea[m] of light over a range of 800 feet. The case is tubular in shape an[d] is made of fibre with all fittings in beautiful nickel plate. It em[bodies] all Bond features—shock absorber, three-way switch, lon[g] life. Truly a value hard to duplicate at anywhere near our lo[w] price. Complete with lamp, measures 9⅝x2⅝ inches.

No. 6 E 3205—Bond Focusing Searchlight. Each, 1.42.
Less 2%. Net.... **1.3**

Bond's Candelite Candle

Lights and Extinguishes Automatically

Suitable for Every Home

One of the handiest devices made for convenience and safety in home auxiliary lighting. Developed in modernistic design, it is extremely attractive, harmonizing with the furnishings of boudoir, guest room and nursery. Also can be used for night light, telephone light. Makes an ideal prize at bridge parties or may be offered as a gift item. Put it down, it goes out—lift it up and it lights up—absolutely automatically. Finished in satin brass. Height, 7⅛ inches; width 3⅛ inches. Uses two life long Bond mono-cells.

No. 2059. Candelite Flashlight Candle. Less mono-cells. Each.... **36c**

Original 1931 Catalog Page.

Original 1935 Catalog Page.

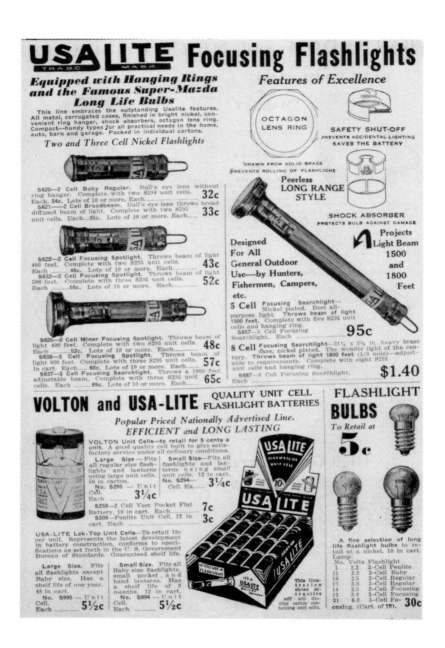

Original 1935 Catalog Page.

USA-LITE FLASHLIGHT DEALS

Startling New Display and Greatly Improved Quality

The USA LITE Self-Selling System includes the attractive display racks illustrated below (made of heavy blue alligator leatheroid) with handsome descriptive card (in gold, red, white and blue), delivered to your store with flashlights already mounted. No fussing with folds or tabs; just remove rack from carton, display with card in your window and on your counter and watch 'em come a-running. Here is the answer to the challenge of competition—greater value, easier selling, better profit margins—certainly a very satisfactory combination.

Usalite Deal No. 4

WHAT YOU GET: 6—2-cell Broad Beam Flashlights already mounted on display rack, including descriptive price card, complete with USA LITE LOK TOP Batteries and Genuine MAZDA Bulbs, at 49c each retail $2.94
36 extra USA LITE LOK TOP Batteries in display carton, at 10c each retail 3.60

Total Selling Value $6.54
WHAT IT COSTS YOU **$4.45**
(Leaves you a gross profit of $2.09)
S2567—49c Flashlight Deal (Mfrs. 4)

Usalite Deal No. 5

WHAT YOU GET: 6—2-cell Focusing Spotlights already mounted on display rack, including descriptive price card, complete with USA LITE LOK TOP Batteries and Genuine MAZDA Bulbs, at 59c each retail $3.54
36 extra USA LITE LOK TOP Batteries in display carton, at 10c each retail 3.60

Total Selling Value $7.14
WHAT IT COSTS YOU **$5.06**
(Leaves you a gross profit of $2.08)
S2568—59c Flashlight Deal (Mfrs. 5)

Usalite Deal No. 9

WHAT YOU GET: 3—2-cell Focusing Searchlights already mounted on display rack, including descriptive price card, complete with USA LITE LOK TOP Batteries and Genuine MAZDA Bulbs, at 98c each retail $2.94
39 extra USA LITE LOK TOP Batteries in display carton, at 10c each retail 3.90

Total Selling Value $6.84
WHAT IT COSTS YOU **$4.57**
(Leaves you a gross profit of $2.27)
S2569—98c Flashlight Deal (Mfrs. 9)

Usalite Deal No. 14

WHAT YOU GET: 3—5-cell Focusing Searchlights already mounted on display rack, including descriptive price card, complete with USA LITE LOK TOP Batteries and Genuine MAZDA Bulbs, at 1.49 each retail $4.47
33 extra USA LITE LOK TOP Batteries in display carton, at 10c each retail 3.30

Total Selling Value $7.77
WHAT IT COSTS YOU **$5.07**
(Leaves you a gross profit of $2.70)
S2570—$1.49 Flashlight Deal (Mfrs. 14)

Original 1935 Catalog Page.

You Make More Than 50% Profit, Too

—On Less Than $5.00 Investment.
Never Before Has An Offer Been Made to Beat This

We were fortunate to tie up with the maker of Kwik-lite products so as to secure this special "give away deal" for our dealers. In this deal the merchant can actually give his customer a flashlight lantern free. When giving these lanterns away, you sell as accessories to operate them 24 of the 48 cells (two for each lantern) and 12 of the 24 bulbs (one for each lantern) and the remaining 24 cells and bulbs are sold as renewals. Here is where you gain your profit. Simple, isn't it, and what a tremendous "wallop" such an appeal has in making sales for you. The lantern will throw a light 350 feet or can be made to spread its illumination for close up lighting. Size 3½x2x3½ in. and furnished attractively in assorted silver, red and green. Deal consists of the following:

12 Kwik-lite Focusing Lanterns (no charge)
48 Kwik-lite Double Life Batteries
24 Kwik-lite Meter Tested Bulbs
Advertising helps are included free with each deal.

Complete Deal Only.... **$4.92**

JUNIORlite

Electric Lantern
A Brand NEW Fast-Selling Item

Throws a beam of light 600 Feet. Has all-around Spreadlight top.

A sensation—of course you'll admit it's a wonder when you see how much you get for so little money. Combines in its peerless design utility features for every imagined kind of lighting — spot beam from front reflector projecting a stream of light 600 feet! — for all around spread illumination in camps, cabin, barn or other outbuildings on the farm — anywhere a safe efficient light may be required. It's the "Ace" of small, compact electric lanterns — smartly styled in silver color and bright trim, standing 4½ in. high. Takes two standard 1¼-inch flashlight cells.

"2 REFLECTOR LANTERN"
2 Std. 1¼" CELLS-HEIGHT 4¼ WIDTH 3½

S5079L—Delta Juniorlite Electric Lantern, complete with batteries. Each................ **$1.10**

Delta Flashlight Lanterns

The "MARIONETTE"—Retail Price 39c, Less Batteries

The Marionette Pocket Lantern. All metal case finished in lustrous red, green or black; small, compact, fits in hand, vest pocket or lady's purse, operates on 2 standard unit cells.
S5078—Size 3¼x2⅜x1¼ in., 6 on display card, asst. 2 of each color. Card of 6 (Complete with Batteries)......$2.40
S5079—Without Unit Cells.
Card...................................$1.80
S994—Extra Unit Cells. Each.....05½

The Sportsman's New Sensational
DRY CELL LANTERN

A new style amazingly useful electric lantern adaptable to scores of needs. Campers, tourists, farmers and all kinds of outdoor and night workers, in homes, cabins, stores — everywhere the "Red" Guard fits in for useful service. Can be placed in practically any desired position to direct its illumination where needed most. Built rugged to give years of service. Takes four standard size flashlight batteries. Finished in red with handle and base cadmium plated, creating a very pleasing contrast.

S1776—Red Guard Dry Cell Lantern. Each................................... **65c**

S995—Batteries for above. Ea. 5½c

This Fine Flashlight FREE

With Order for Box of 36 "Kwiklite" Flashlight Batteries

Unusual profits are available through this special battery deal. It includes one chrome plated focusing flashlight FREE with each box of 36 Kwiklite double life cell flashlight batteries. Sell the batteries at 10 cents each and get your usual profit, the sale of the flashlight at 75 cents adds to your net gain.

Complete Deal With FREE FLASHLIGHT **$2.34**

S5040—Kwiklite Battery Deal. Complete...

LATEST
Sportsman's Focusing Dry Cell Lantern
An Incomparable value. Throws a beam of light 800 ft.

Useful to the sportsman, farmer, laborer and in a great number of situations where its bright illumination will help out in trouble, changing a tire or fixing something that must be repaired at once. Sturdy steel body — good for unlimited years of dependable service. Focus easily and instantly adjustable by screw in back—from piercing beam to broad spread light. Nail notch in back of top handle permits hanging lantern up in safe, convenient position. Rich red enamel finish, bright polished reflector 4½ in. diameter, non-tarnishing. Scientific design, automotive type switch conveniently mounted on back for quick easy control. Operates on 2 standard No. 6 dry cells. One pair of fresh batteries good for 5 months to a year without change.

S1777—New Apollo Dry Cell Lantern. Each................................ **$1.20**
S995—Batteries for above. Each....20c

Original 1935 Catalog Page.

EVEREADY FLASHLIGHTS

Girl Scout Flashlight

No.	Size	Finish	Retail	Our List Each
2664	6x1¾	Jade Green	$1.05	$1.36

Requires 2 No. 935 Unit Cells. Lamp No. 1161.

Industrial Flashlight

No.	Size	Finish	Retail Price	Our List Price Each
3251	8"x2"	Black	$1.75	$2.40

Requires 2 No. 950 Unit Sells. Lamp No. 1191 Special.

No.	Size	Finish	Retail	Our List Each
2663	6x1¾	Chromium	$1.95	$1.36

Requires 2 No. 935 Unit Cells. Lamp No. 1161.

No.	Size	Finish	Retail	Our List Each
2604	6¾x1½	Black	$0.75	$0.98

Requires 2 No. 950 Unit Cells. Lamp No. 1161.

No.	Size	Finish	Retail	Our List Each
2671	7¾x1½	Black	$1.05	$1.38

Requires 2 No. 950 Unit Cells. Lamp No. 1161.

No.	Size	Finish	Retail	Our List Each
2619	8½x1½	Black	$1.45	$1.88

Requires 3 No. 950 Unit Cells. Lamp No. 1162.

NOTE—Price does not include Unit Cells. Only case and lamp.

Searchlight Types

No.	Size	Finish	Retail	Our List Each
2672	9¼x1½	Black	$1.45	$1.88

Requires 3 No. 950 Unit Cells. Lamp No. 1162.

Focusing Spotlight with 800-Foot Range

No.	Size	Finish	Retail	Our List Each
2642	10x1½	Black	$2.20	$2.86

Requires 3 No. 950 Unit Cells. Lamp No. 1162.

The New Eveready
5-CELL FOCUSING FLASHLIGHT
"The Searchlight of Flashlights"

No. 2645

The most powerful Flashlight ever offered. When properly focused, this flashlight will throw a clear, sharp beam of light over three times as far as any flashlight now on the market. Furnished in Chromium Finish only.

No.	Size	Finish	Retail	Our List Each
2645	14½x1½	Chromium	$2.50	$3.26

Requires 5 No. 950 Cells. Lamp No. 1168.

NEW EVEREADY BOY SCOUT FLASHLIGHT.

Approved and Endorsed by The Boy Scouts of America.

Eveready No. 2697 is a 2-cell focusing light finished in olive drab and equipped with ring hanger, belt clip and safety-lock switch. It carries the official Boy Scout insignia as evidence of the fact that it is the only flashlight which has received the unqualified endorsement of the Boy Scout organization.

Catalog No.	Finish	Size	List Price Each	Net Price Per Case
2697	Khaki	7x1½	$1.30	$1.68

Requires 2 No. 950 Unit Cells. Lamp No. 1161.

Original 1936 Catalog Page.

Eveready Display Package No. 9

A new display package of low priced Evereadys. Contains three each of three popular types—nine flashlights in all. Display package takes up only six inches of counter space.

No. 9 display package, consisting of 3 No. 250, 3 No. 251 and 3 No. 351 Flashlights (without batteries).
Retail value of flashlights..........................$4.77
Our list price $6.68

Eveready Display Package No. 04

Display No. 04
6 No. 2604 Eveready 2-cell flashlights, shipped in a box which opens up to make this counter display.
List value of flashlights..........................$4.50
Our List Price..................................$5.88

Eveready Electric Candle
French Colonial Design

No. 1653—Electric Candle. Height 7¼ in.; width (at base) 4⅜ in. Uses 2 No. 935 Eveready Batteries. Lamp No. 1173.
List Price, less Batteries.....$1.80
Our List Price, less Batteries.. 2.34

No. 4758
Eveready Wallite

Equipped with Automatic Time Switch. Finished in Ivory. Size 6x4½x2½ in. Uses 3 No. 950 Eveready Batteries. Lamp No. 1167.
List Price, less Batteries........$1.65
Our List Price, less Batteries...... 2.14

A New Portable Flasher

Requires four standard Eveready Columbia 6-inch dry cells connected in series to deliver 6 volts. Extra 6-volt Eveready Mazda lamp No. 1135 inside battery housing. Battery compartment constructed of seamless steel attractively finished in red. Top of flasher cadmium plated for weather protection. Heavy Fresnel type red glass lens. Padlock for battery compartment with an extra long hasp so that the device can be chained. This flasher is of rugged construction throughout and entirely weather proof.
Our List Price.................$30.00

Eveready Display Package No. 71

6 No. 2671 Eveready 2-cell focusing flashlights, shipped in a box which opens up to make this counter display.
List value of flashlights ..$6.30
Our list price..$8.16

Display No. 71

H. B. Safety Night Light

A light all night at little or no cost for electricity. Burns 100 hours for about 1c. Operates on 110 volts A. C. 60 cycle.
Our list price, each....................$1.30
Shipping wt., ½ lb. each.

Original 1936 Catalog Page.

WINCHESTER FLASHLIGHTS
FLASHLIGHT DISPLAY UNITS

Consists of six No. 0 8 1 8 spotlights with 500 foot range; 6¾ x 2 inch case; uses two standard batteries and No. PR-2 G. E. Mazda lamp. Put up in a new SI-ME Twin display that can be set up back-to-back or fanned open to full view as illustrated.

Without Batteries
Retail Price (without barteries) $1.15
No. D0818 ....Each **$10.30**
Weight each, 3¾ lbs.; one in a carton.

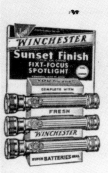

Consists of three No. 0828 spotlights with 600 foot range; 9x2¼ inch case; uses three standard batteries and 1 No. PR-3 G. E. Mazda lamp.

Put up on a new and attractive SI-ME ladder display as illustrated.

Without Batteries
Retail (without batteries) $1.35
No. D0828 .... Each **$6.05**
Wgt. each, 2½ lbs.; one in a carton.

Consists of eight streamlined pocket light pen-lights, four No. 6610 brass, chromium plated and four No. 6618 solid 22K copper pen-lights with simple, easy-to-operate, fool-proof switches; uses No. 222 Mazda magnifying lamp.

Mounted on an attractive counter display, 10 inches high and 10 inches wide.

Without Batteries
Total Retail Value (Without Batteries) $3.92
Retail Price (Complete with Batteries) $0.59
No. D-6610 ....Each **$5.65**
Weight each, 14 ozs.; one in a carton.

FLASHLIGHT LENSES

WINCHESTER
Assortments

An attractive lens display assortment requiring little counter space but renders a complete flashlight service to your customers.

Contents
Contains 36 double thickness f l a s h l i g h t lenses—30 spotlight size 1⅜ in. diameter and 6 searchlight size 3⅛ in. diameter.

Total Retail Value, $3.60
No. L1045....Ea. **$2.10**
Weight each, 2 lbs.; one in a carton.

FLASHLIGHT CLAMPS

WINCHESTER
Clamps on Automobile Steering Column

Substantially constructed of steel, highly polished nickel plated finish; holds any standard flashlight and clamps on steering column without the use of any tools.

No. 1037 ....Each **$0.25**
Weight each, 3 oz.; packed loose.

ELECTRIC LANTERNS

WINCHESTER
TWIN SERVICE HEADLIGHT
Cases and Lamps Less Batteries

Combines four lights of genuine convenience. Fitting easily over the head it can be used for a long range focusing headlight or for a diffusing light that puts a broad field of illumination just where it is wanted; light that moves with every turn of the head and yet leaves both hands free. Or it can be carried by convenient bail handle as a hand lantern, either focusing or diffusing; or worn on the belt where it is held by spring clasp on back of case; lens can be tilted up or down as desired; has a range of 700 feet; uses three standard batteries and No. 13 Mazda bulb; fitted with adjustable elastic head band; black finish case with chromium plated trim; 4x2¾x1¼ inch case; 1¾ inch lens.

No. 7924—Black with chromium trim..Each **$2.95 4.25**
Weight each, 15 ozs.; one in a carton.

Original 1939 Catalog Page.

WINCHESTER FLASHLIGHTS
FLASHLIGHT AND BATTERY DISPLAY DEALS

Solid Copper

Consists of six 6½ x 1⅞ in. two cell focusing spotlights and 48 No. 1511 batteries. Cases are made from seamless 22K. copper; positive lock "off" and "on" switch with new guard rail; recessed octagon non-rolling lens ring; candle light feature; brilliant reflector; No. 14 Mazda bulb.

With 48 No. 1511 Batteries

Retail Value—6 flashlights and 48 batteries......$7.14
Retail Price complete with batteries $0.59
No. K59 ....Each **$10.50**
Weight each, 14 lbs.; packed in two cartons.

Solid Brass; Full Chromium Finish

Consists of six No. 5810 focusing spotlights and forty-eight No. 1511 batteries; cases are equipped with new type positive 3-position safety lock switch, shock absorber non-rolling recessed lens ring, candle light feature, genuine Mazda bulbs and folding ring hangers; 6¾ x 2 inch case; mounted on an attractive Si-Me Twin display stand.

Retail Value—6 No. 5810 flashlights and 48 batteries $8.70

(Suggested retail complete with batteries 85c each.)

No. 85 ....Each **$12.45**
Weight each, 14 lbs.; packed in two cartons.

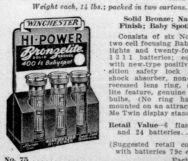

Solid Bronze; Natural Finish; Baby Spotlights.

Consists of six No. 5517 two cell focusing Baby Spotlights and twenty-four No. 1311 batteries; equipped with new-type positive 3-position safety lock switch, shock absorber, non-rolling recessed lens ring, candlelite feature, genuine Mazda bulbs, (No ring hanger); mounted on an attractive Si-Me Twin display stand.

Retail Value—6 flashlights and 24 batteries...$5.94

(Suggested retail complete with batteries 79c each.)

No. 75 ....Each **$8.50**
Weight each, 4½ lbs.; packed in two cartons.

WINCHESTER FLASHLIGHTS
FLASHLIGHT AND BATTERY DISPLAY DEALS

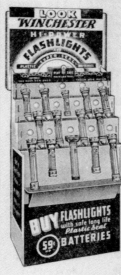

Consists of twenty-four "Hi-Power" flashlight cases, 14 streamlined design and 10 standard styles, 96 No. 1511 Super-Seal batteries.

With each deal the floor merchandiser display rack is given free. Displays 14 different flashlight models on three tiers, top shelf displays 48 flashlight batteries and 60 flashlight lamps; space on right side of display for installing lamp and battery tester; ample storage space in rear for extra stock.

Size of display, height 53 inches; width, 21 inches; depth, 12 inches; finely lithographed in four colors, attractively lettered. Lamp and battery tester included without charge.

Deal Contains

			Retail Each
5	No. 9818	2-cell 22K Copper Spotlights........	$0.59
2	No. 5517	2-cell Baby Bronzelite Spotlights....	.79
3	No. 9810	2-cell Chrome Spotlights	.79
2	No. 9929	3-cell Chrome and Black Searchlights	.89
4	No. 1818	2-cell 22K Copper Fixt-Focus Spotlights.................................	.98
2	No. 1814	2-cell Chrome and Copper Fixt-Focus Spotlights..................	.98
2	No. 0810	2-cell Deluxe Chrome Fixt-Focus Spotlights	1.35
2	No. 0818	2-cell "Sunset" Finish DeLuxe Fixt-Focus Spotlights	1.35
1	No. 0820	3-cell Chrome DeLuxe Fixt-Focus Spotlight	1.65
1	No. 0828	3-cell DeLuxe "Sunset" Finish Fixt-Focus Spotlight	1.65
96	No. 1511	Winchester Plastic "Super Seal" Flashlight Batteries—10c each..........	9.60

Total Retail Value $27.66

No. 1121 ....Each **$40.60**
Weight each, 42½ lbs.; packed in three cartons.

Original 1939 Catalog Page.

ELECTRIC LANTERNS

DELTA, SILVERLITE
600 Foot Range.

Steel battery case, durable silver enamel. Silver plated brass conic shaped reflector. Extra heavy 2½ inch convexed lens; automotive type switch.
Top bail has nail hook for hanging; two folding handles in rear provide easy carrying or wearing on belt.
Operates on two No. BG1950 standard flashlight cells and No. 14 bulbs.

Price does not include Batteries. Each
No. 9DSL—Silver gray. Height 3¾ ins; width 3 ins; depth 1¾ ins; wt each 1 lb................. 2 01
$1 00
One in carton, 12 in shipping carton.

HUSKY

Steel case, crimped base, red enameled finish; 7 inches high, 5¾ inches wide, 3 inches thick.
Operates on two No. 6 dry cell batteries. Black composition slide switch.
Fitted with focusing device in back of case. Nickel aluminum alloy reflector; 4¼ inch extra heavy lens. Fitted with detachable wire bail and handle on back.

Price does not include Batteries. Each
No. D75—Less batteries, with No. 35 bulb............ 3 00
$1 55
One in carton, 12 in stand pkg; wt each 1½ lbs.

DELTA, RED BIRD
With Dual-Reflection.

Bright red enamel finish with chrome trimmings. Accommodates two standard No. 6 dry cell batteries.
Dual-reflection is a combination of two reflectors producing two light results, either on 800 foot penetrating beam or perfect shadowless spread. Control lever in base.
Two handles in back which fold flat against case when not in use, also equipped with carrying bail. Switch in back of case for turning off and on.

Price does not include Batteries. Each
No. 10RB—Size case 7¾ ins high by 6½ ins wide by 3¾ ins deep. With No. 35 bulb 4 50
$2 25
One in carton, 12 in stand pkg; wt each 2¼ lbs.

DELTA—APOLLO
External Focus—800 Foot Beam.

Sturdy steel body; comfortable rigid top handle, red enamel finish; bright polished, non-tarnishing reflector. Automotive type switch mounted on back.
Height body 7½ inches, over all 10 inches; width 5½ inches.
Focus quickly adjusted from piercing beam to broad spread light.
Operates on two No. 66 Blue Grass or two No. 6 Columbia dry cell batteries.

Price does not include Batteries. Each
No. 10NA—Diam reflector 4½ ins............ 3 90 $1 95
One in carton, 12 in shipment carton; wt each 2½ lbs.

ELECTRIC LANTERNS

DELTA POWERLITE

Beautiful silver enameled body, bright trim; 800 foot spot beam front, floodlight top; both lights under instant fingertip control from same switch.
Bail reverses for floodlight down, also hangs by bail and hooks over nail in wall.
Operates on standard 6 volt No. 123 battery; 80 to 100 hours battery life.
Height body 6½ inches; diameter body 3⅜ inches.

Price does not include Battery. Each
No. DA1530—Diam front reflector 4½ ins; diam top 3 ins................ $6 69
One in carton; wt each 2½ lbs.

DELTA-JUNIORLITE—2 REFLECTOR DESIGN
600 Foot Range.

Heavy gauge steel, silver finish; bright plated trim. Silver plated brass front reflector. White enameled top reflector.
Two reflectors; side reflector offers a penetrating spot beam of 600 feet.
Top reflector offers a wide diffused spread or floodlight. Two lights operate from same batteries instantly from single, double-acting three-position switch, but only one may be operated at a time.
Top bail has notch for hanging. Two folding handles in rear for easy carrying or wearing on belt.

Operates on two No. BG2950 Blue Grass batteries, and No. 14 Mazda bulb.
Size case, height 4¾ inches; width 3⅛ inches.

Price does not include Batteries.
No......................... 1JL
Each......................... 3 51
$1 90
One in carton, 12 in stand pkg; wt each 1 lb.

DELTA-WILDCAT

Steel case, sturdily constructed, attractive silver finish; octagon shape base with flat sides; comfortable hand-conforming handle, punched on ends and top for hanging on cord or nail.
Double acting switch for finger-tip control of both floodlight and spot beam.
Floodlight brilliantly illuminates a 20 foot circle.
Operates on standard 1¼ inch flashlight cells, either 2 or 4; 8 to 10 hours on 2 cells, 20 to 24 hours on 4 cells.

Price does not include Batteries. Each
No. 1WCL—Height not including handle 4¾ ins; diam reflector 2⅜ ins $3 03
One in carton; wt each 1¼ lbs.

Original 1939 Catalog Page.

FLASHLIGHT ASSORTMENTS
EVEREADY
2-CELL AUTOMATIC SPOTLIGHTS

Contains 6 No. 2251, 2 cell spotlights. Seamless brass tube, chromium finish with rolled on black decoration.

Uses 2 regular size batteries and Lamp No. PR2.

D96-25-6—Less batteries............Ass't $24 57
One ass't in shp ctn; wt ass't 11 lbs. $11 70

FLASHLIGHT ASSORTMENTS
EVEREADY—TORCH LIGHT

Safety red glow lite visible for ½ mile.
Prefocused piercing white beam. Unbreakable red glow wand.
Heavy gauge seamless metal case.
Jumbo switch.
Uses 2 regular size "D" batteries and D96-PR2 bulb. Length case 6 inches.
Assortment consists of six torch-lites, three each D96-2T3 and D96-2T5.

D96-35-TL
Ass't $16 62 $8 04
One asst in shp ctn; wt ass't 2⅜ lbs.

OPEN STOCK
Uses D96-FLL-1 lens.
D96-2 T3—3-inch wand.......Each $2 87 $1 39
D96-2 T5—5-inch wand.......Each 3 06 1 49
24 in shp ctn; wt ctn 9 lbs.

EVEREADY PENLITES

Display contains two different styles; one is all chrome, the other black and chrome. Diameter ½ inch, length 4¹³⁄₁₆ inches.
Uses two No. AAA batteries.
Less batteries.

D96-21
Ass't $24 57 $11 76
One ass't in shp ctn.

EVEREADY
Seven For The Price Of Six

Polished chrome all-metal case.
Knurled barrel for safe, sure grip.
Dependable switch.
Built-in lamp protector.
Display contains 3 red, 2 yellow, 2 turquoise.

D96-27
Display $15 51
12 in shp ctn; $ 8 33
wt display 25 lbs.

EVEREADY— BEACON LITE
Unbreakable safety glow lens ring.
Heavy gauge metal case with durable finish. Jumbo switch, unbreakable polyethylene cap.
Use lamp No. D96-PR2 and two regular size "D" batteries.
Assortment consists of:
3—Copper "Beacon" lites
4—Chrome "Beacon" lites

D96-20
Ass't $18 33 $9 03
One ass't in shp ctn;
wt ass't 3 lbs.

EVEREADY MAGNET LITE
3-Cell

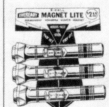

Powerful Alnico type magnet switch, with powerful 18 pound pull, holds fast to steel.
Heavy gauge metal, chrome plated.
Unbreakable safety glass head with lamy shock absorber.
Uses D96-PR3 bulb and 2 standard size D flashlight batteries.
Assortment consists of 3 No. 3-7MF Magnet lites and 1 free displayer.

D96-3-7MF—Less batteries...........Ass't $15 69
12 ass'ts in shp ctn; wt ass't 18 lbs. $ 7 47

Original 1961 Catalog Page.

ELECTRIC FLASHLIGHT ASSORTMENTS
JEWELITES
One-Cell Flashlight.

Includes 12 flashlights, three each, four different finishes: mandarin red, apple green, chrome yellow and nickel plated.

The head piece is moulded from a translucent material which matches finish on the body. A turn of the head piece releases a brilliant beam of light which penetrates in much the same manner as a focusing spotlight.

Small enough to be carried in vest pocket or ladies purse. Requires one penlite style 103 unit cell and 1.2 volt, No. 112 bulb.

Complete With Batteries.

Per Ass't of 12
No. 12M—Length 3 ins; diam ⅝ in........... 6 60
$0 29
One ass't in three color counter display stand; wt ass't 1 lb.

BOND, STYLO CASES
2 Cell Focusing Spotlight.

Solid brass case, heavily pre-chromed all over before baked finish is applied. Ultra-modern two color designs enriched with brilliant chromium p l a t e d bands. Two each of ivory, maroon and blue. Positive 3-way safety lock switch, spare bulb carrier, recessed hanger, octagonal non-rolling l e n s ring, bevelled plate glass lens, brilliant silver plated reflector, original candle light feature. Uses No. BG1950 batteries.

Batteries not included.

Per Ass't of 6
No. 600—Wt ass't 3½ lbs........... $13 80
One ass't in carton.

BOND
Solid brass case, full chromuim plated. Two cell focusing; octagon lens ring.

Assortment includes twelve flashlights and 48 No. 102 Bond super-service mono-cells.

Per Ass't of 12
No. 390—Wt ass't 4½ lbs........... $14 28
Packed in dual displays of 6 each in one carton.

ELECTRIC FLASHLIGHT ASSORTMENTS
BOND BRONZ-LITE
Solid Bronze Case.

Two Cell Focusing.

Solid golden bronze case, with built-in shock absorber, candle light feature, folding end-cap hanger, 3-way lock switch, silvered mirror reflector and bevelled plate glass lens.

Includes: 6 flashlights packed in display and 48 only No. 102 Bond Super-Service Mono-Cells.

Per Ass't
No. 980—Wt ass't 10 lbs........... $19 08
One ass't in carton.

BOND FIBRE-BRONZ
Fibre Case, Bronze Fittings.

Two Cell Focusing.

Black corrugated fibre case, golden bronze fittings, has built-in shock absorber, candle light feature, folding end-cap hanger, 3-way lock switch, silvered mirror reflector and bevelled plate glass lens.

Includes: 6 flashlights packed in display and 48 only No. 102 Bond Super-Service Mono-Cells.

Per Ass't
No. 990—Wt ass't 10 lbs........... $19 08
One ass't in carton.

A clean, well lighted store is the best advertisement you can have. Make your store the brightest spot in your town. Light it up and keep it lit. The small additional cost will be easily offset by the additional business you will realize.

Original 1961 Catalog Page.

ELECTRIC LANTERNS

DELTA—POWERLITE
Two purpose lantern with powerful spot beam and red flasher.

Two-tone gray finish aluminum. Bright plated trim.

Operates on standard 6-volt lantern battery.

Front reflector uses No. D96-27 bulb; top reflector uses No. D96-407 flashing bulb.

D96-A1548—Less Battery ....Each $11 70
One in box; 12 in shp ctn; wt each 2½ lbs. $ 6 19

DELTA POWERLITE
Beautiful silver enameled body, bright trim; 800 foot spot beam front, floodlight top; both lights under instant fingertip control from same switch.
Bail reverses for floodlight down.
Operates on standard 6 volt battery.
Height body 6½ inches; diameter body 3¾ inches.
Diameter front reflector 4½ inches; diameter top 3 inches.
Complete with No. D96-502 bulb.

D96-1530—Less battery .....Each $11 61
One in box; wt each 2½ lbs. $ 6 15

DELTA—POWERTOP
All-purpose lantern with adjustable head—at any angle.

Red enamel finish with bright trim. Positive spring latch for opening and closing. Toggle type switch.

Unbreakable plastic type lens. Operates on standard 6-volt lantern battery.

Uses D96-425 bulb.

D96-A2505—Less battery.... Each $8 67
One in box; 12 in shp ctn; wt each 2 lbs. $4 59

DELTA POWERAY
800 Foot Spot Beam

Blue opalescent enamel steel case. Drop wire handles. Highly polished special aluminum alloy reflector.
Operates on standard six volt lantern batteries.
Height with handles down 5½ inches; height overall 6½ inches; depth overall 5½ inches; base 4½ inches.

4½ inch highly polished reflector.
Complete with No. D96-502 bulb.

D96-A1800—Less battery.... Each $6 57
One in box; wt each 2¼ lbs. $3 49

ELECTRIC LANTERNS
DELTA Buddy
Luminous molded plastic switch GLOWS IN THE DARK!
Case is rustproof, die-cast base with a baked red enamel finish steel. Plastic lens. Bail is polished stainless steel.
2¼ inch highly polished reflector throws a wide, night-shattering beam. Operates on two regular size flashlight batteries.

D96-A1000—Less battery_____ Each $4
One in box; wt each 1 lb. $2

HIPWELL—6 VOLT
Unbreakable red safety head and safety reflector give added safety on the highway.
Giant Spot-Flood reflector projects both long-range and wide-angle beam. Bright red body with yellow ends, chrome lens ring, swivel head, and fold-down handles. 3x8 inches, fits glove compartment or tackle box.

Uses one 6-volt lantern battery and D96-PR13 bulb.

D96-870—Less battery .Each $6 63
One in box; wt each 2½ lbs.

JUSTRITE—INTERCEPTOR LANTERN

Uses standard 6 volt lantern battery and Sealed Beam Lamp No. D96-4 6000 candle power, 100 1500 foot beam. Positive action slide switch.
Hinge with tension screw regulates headpiece. Rustproofed steel case gray and yellow chip-proof baked enamel finish. Chrome plated lens ring.
4¼-inch sealed beam lamp can be turned to any angle through a 135° arc.
Fold down handles on case.

D96-2411-1—Less battery .... Each $1
One in box; wt each 2 lbs.

JUSTRITE
Rust-proofed steel case mounted to swivel. High quality baked-on enamel finish. Gray case, red cover.
Brass reflector chrome plated and highly polished.
Diameter 3½ inches.
Twin-bulb sockets mounted on lever controlled slide. Uses two No. 27 bulbs. Protected by heavy 1½ inch cover glass.
Aluminum tubing handle, steel wire base.
Mechanical, sliding switch—slides either bulb into contact position.
Length case from cover glass to bottom cover 6½ inches; height from wire base to top of handle 11¾ inches.
Uses one 6-volt lantern battery.

D96-2142-6—Less battery........... Each $1
One in box; 12 in shp ctn; wt each 2½ lbs.

Original 1961 Catalog Page.

Original 1931 Catalog Page.

WINCHESTER

No. 60 Winchester Deal

Consists of: New **FREE** Patented SI-ME Twin Display containing 6 of the popular No. 4817 2-cell Bronzelite Spotlights (Solid Bronze) in this new type display, and 48 No. 1511 Winchester Hi-Power Super Seal Unit Cells.

Priced to Retail complete............99c.

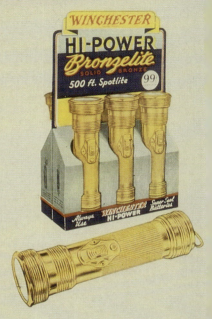

* * *

No. 4817 Winchester Hi-Power 2-cell Bronzelite Spotlight made from SOLID Golden Bronze—a quick seller with great "eye value." Equipped with positive 3-position Safety Lock Switch — Integral Shock Absorber protects bulb. Candle-light feature. Octagon, non-rolling Recessed Lens Ring for lens protection. Folding ring hanger. Silvered reflector. Mazda Bulb No. 14.

No. 75 Winchester Deal

Consists of: New **FREE** patented SI-ME Twin Display containing 6 No. 5517 2-cell Baby Bronzelite Spotlights (SOLID BRONZE) and 24 No. 1311 Winchester Hi-Power Super Seal Unit Cells.

Priced to Retail complete............79c.

* * *

No. 5517 Winchester, brand new Hi-Power 2-cell Baby Bronzelite Spotlight is of a handsome design that will speed up your turnover. It is of Solid Bronze, with the other features that have made the standard size No. 4817 Bronzelite such a fast seller. (No ring hanger).

Unique new patented SI-ME twin displays are counter-space savers. Can be set up side-by-side or back-to-back.

Original 1938 Catalog Page.

WINCHESTER

No. 70 Winchester Deal

No. 4827 Winchester 3-cell focusing Bronzelite Spotlight (made from SOLID Golden Bronze). Designed for quick eye appeal. Equipped with a positive 3-position Safety Lock Switch—Integral Shock Absorber protects bulb. Candle-light feature. Octagon non-rolling Recessed Lens Ring for lens protection. Folding ring hanger. Silvered reflector. Mazda Bulb No. 13.

No. 70 Deal, consisting of *six* No. 4827 3-cell Bronzelites, packed in this FREE Display, and 48 No. 1511 Winchester Hi-Power Super Seal Unit Cells. Priced to retail complete $1.29.

WINCHESTER

Twin Service Headlight Lanterns

Light Where You Want It With Both Hands Free

The Winchester Twin-Service Headlight Lantern combines four lights of genuine convenience. Fitting easily over the head it can be used for a long range focusing headlight or for a diffusing light that puts a broad field of illumination just where it is wanted—light that moves with every turn of the head and yet leaves both hands free. Or it can be carried by its convenient bail handle as an electric hand lantern—again either focusing or diffusing.

Made in two styles, No. 7924, three cell, and No. 79124, five cell. Both styles are equipped with silver mirror reflectors (for long range focusing) and a matted finished reflector for spreadlight service.

No. 79124

No. 79124, 5-cell Headlight Lantern with focusing reflector has a range of 2500 ft. Black finish case with chromium plated trim. Uses 5 No. 1511 Winchester Hi-Power Super Seal Unit Cells and Mazda Super Bulb No. 605.

Retail Price (without batteries) . . . $4.50 each

No. 7924

No. 7924, 3-cell Headlight Lantern with focusing reflector has a range of 700 ft. Black finish case with chromium plated trim. Uses 3 No. 1511 Winchester Hi-Power Super Seal Unit Cells and Mazda Bulb No. 13.

Retail Price (without batteries) . . . $2.95 each

Original 1938 Catalog Page.

WINCHESTER

HI-POWER SUPER SEAL FLASHLIGHT BATTERIES

PATENTED SUPER SEAL →

Winchester HI-POWER Super Seal Flashlight Batteries give high illuminating output and longer brilliant life. The moulded Super Seal is spun down firmly under the zinc container edge and tightly seals under pressure an insulating washer soaked in paraffine against the shoulder of the container. This prevents power loss—insures supreme service.

ALWAYS FRESH EVERYONE DATED →

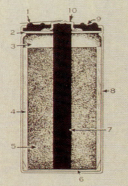

Winchester batteries have exceptional recuperative quality—up to 120% more in total minutes of service and continue to recuperate up to twice as many days as other types of cells when discharged continuously to a specified voltage, with this discharge repeated daily.

Features of battery as shown in cut open section illustrated at left— 1—Top shaped to prevent accidental short circuit. 2—Waterproof washer protects cap from corrosion and forms tight seal. 3—Air to allow expansion of gases and spent electrolite. 4—Electrolytic paste through which current passes. 5—Depolarizing mixture, keeps voltage high. 6—Cupped bottom washer centralizes core and insulates bottom of zinc container, preventing corrosive action. 7—Carbon rod or positive electrode. 8—Seamless zinc container—acts as negative electrode. 9—Super seal insulator top of moulded material. 10—Brass contact cap, nickel plated and formed around edge of hole making tight seal.

* * *

These Winchester Switches Do Their Own Thinking

(At right top)—3 position Safety Lock switch which provides most effectively against accidental battery discharge. Designed for supremely long service in the hardest use. To depress flash button to make electric contact—move thumb slide forward 1 safety click. Two forward clicks of the thumb slide give a permanent electric contact. When thumb slide is withdrawn 2 clicks the flash button at bottom is locked rigidly in position thus preventing accidental discharge. Thumb slide and flash button in this switch operate on 2 separate internal connections thus giving positive control of the electric power of the light. →

(At right bottom)—This is also a 3 position Safety Lock switch which has been produced to insure long and satisfactory service that will equal the best of competitive switches. In this switch the flash button makes contact only when the thumb slide has been unlocked by 1 forward motion click. When thumb slide is moved forward 2 clicks steady light is obtained. When the thumb slide is brought back 2 full clicks the flash button is automatically locked. →

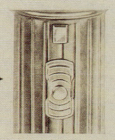

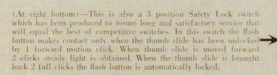

Original 1938 Catalog Page.

Original 1939 Catalog Page.

Original 1950 Catalog Page.

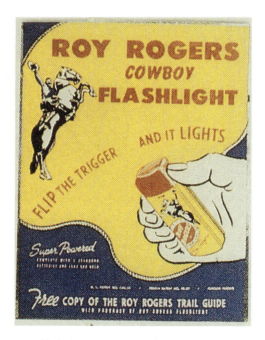

Original 1950 Catalog Page.

Flashlights (a - z)

(From Left to Right)
(1) American -1920, 5 1/2"
$25+

(2) American -1934, 5 1/2"
$15+

(3) Anglo - American Co -1925, 8 3/4"
$20+

(From Top to Bottom)
(1) Aurora -1936, 5 1/2"
$5+

(2) Ashflash - Three color flashlight with rear blinker. 1955, 9"
$25+

(3) Ashflash -1950, 7"
$5+

(From Left to Right)
(1) Belknap - 1939, 9 1/2"
$15+

(2) Blaco "Stylemaster" - 1939, 7 3/4"
$10+

(3) BMG "Girl Scouts" - 1969, 7 1/2"
$5+

(4) BMG "U.S.N. Beacon Light" - 1942, 3 3/4"
$10+

(From Left to Right)
(1) Bond - 1939, 6 1/2"
$10+

(2) Boy Scouts of America - 1947, 7 1/2"
$15+

(3) Bright Star - 1932, 6 1/4"
$10+

(4) Bright Star "Trafficmaster" - 1939, 7"
$15+

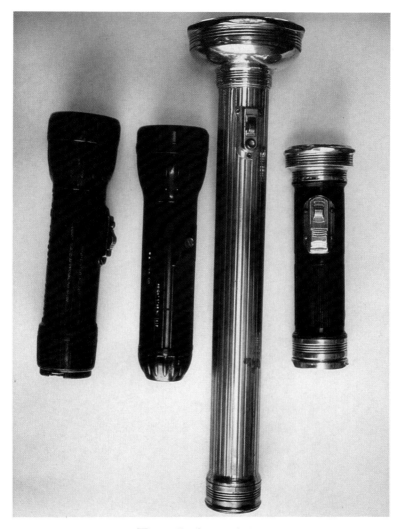

(From Left to Right)
(1) Bright Star "Coast Guard" - 1939, 8"
$20+

(2) Bright Star "B&O. R.R. Co." - No. 1618, 1939, 7"
$35+

(3) Bright Star - 1946, 14 1/2"
$15+

(4) Bright Star - 1952, 6 3/4"
$10+

(From Left to Right)
(1) Burgess -1930, 6 1/2"
$30+

(2) Burgess -1935, 6 1/2"
$25+

(3) Burgess -1938, 6 1/4"
$25+

(4) Burgess -1950,   6 3/4"
$20+

(5) Burgess -1939, 5 5/8"
$30+

Burgess - Two cell flashlight & box
Model #452, 1945, 7"
$10+

Burgess, 1933
21 1/4"
$20+

Burgess - 3 cell prefocused
spotlight & box. Model #446
1950, 9"   **$10+**

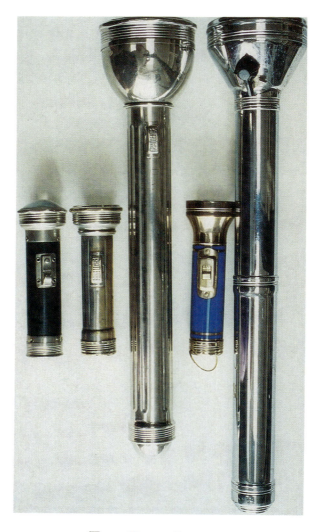

(From Top to Bottom)

(1) Case Tested - Fiber Walled with Bullseye Lens, 1926, 5 1/2" **$30+**

(2) Challenge - Brass Constructed, 1933, 5 1/2" – **$15+**

(3) Challenge - Aluminum Constructed, 1946, 15" – **$10+**

(4) Official Cub Scout Flashlight - Brass Constructed, 1955, 5 1/2" **$15+**

(5) Duo Tint - 3 or 6 Cell Aluminum Flashlight, 1948, 17" – **$20+**

(From Left to Right)
(1) Eveready - Fiber Walled with Bullseye Lens.
1912, 6 5/8"
$25+

(2) Eveready - Fiber Walled with Bullseye Lens.
1913, 5 1/2"
$25+

(3) Eveready "Daylo" - Aluminum Constructed.
1915, 5 1/2"
$20+

(From Left to Right)
(1) Eveready "Daylo" - Aluminum Constructed.
1915, 9"
$25+

(2) Eveready "Daylo" - Fiber Walled.
1917, 9"
$25+

(3) Eveready "Daylo" - Fiber Walled.
1920, 6 3/8"
$20+

(From Left to Right)
(1) Eveready "Daylo" - Fiber Walled with Bullseye Lens.
1922, 6 1/2"
$15+

(2) Eveready - Aluminum Constructed.
1923, 6 1/8"
$15+

(3) Eveready - No. 2602, Aluminum Constructed.
1925, 5 1/2"
$20+

(4) Eveready - No. 2660, Aluminum Constructed.
1925, 5 1/2"
$15+

(From Left to Right)
(1) Eveready "Official Boy Scouts of America"- Plastic Constructed.
No. 2697, 1938, 7 1/2"
$15+

(2) Eveready - Aluminum Constructed.
1939, 7 1/8"
$5+

(3) Eveready "Masterlite" - Aluminum with Green Paint.
1948, 7"
$5+

(4) Eveready "Masterlite" - Aluminum with Black Paint.
1948, 7"
$5+

(From Left to Right)
(1) Eveready - No. 2645.
Aluminum Constructed.
1926, 14 3/8"
$10+

(2) Eveready "U.S.N."
Aluminum with Bullseye Lens.
1927, 6 7/8"
$25+

  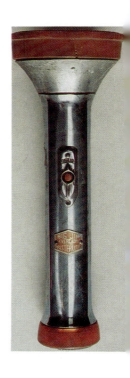

(1) Eveready "Gaslight Torch" - Brass Constructed. No. 3266, 1931, 10", (Made in England)
$50+

(2) Eveready - Aluminum with Bullseye Lens. No. 2604, 1925, 7"
$15+

(3) Eveready "Big Jim Masterlite" - Aluminum Constructed, 1961, 10"
$10+

(From Left to Right)
(1) Flash - Scope - Aluminum Constructed.
Flashlight and Telescope Combo Made by The Pitney Speciality Device Company.
1929, 8 5/8"
$30+

(2) Franco - Fiber Walled with Bullseye Lens.
1912, 5 3/8"
$20+

(3) Franco - Fiber Walled with Bullseye Lens.
1915, 6 3/4"
$20+

(4) Franco - Fiber Walled with Bullseye Lens.
1922, 9"
$30+

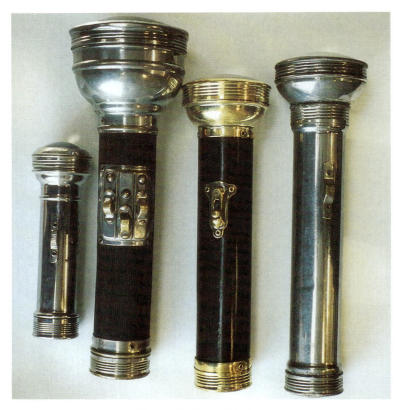

(From Left to Right)
(1) Franco - Aluminum with Bullseye Lens.
1925, 5 3/4"
$15+

(2) Franco - Fiber Walled with Bullseye Lens.
Has Unique 3 - Way Switch.
1930, 10"
$25+

(3) French Ray-o-Lite - Fiber Walled with Bullseye Lens.
1913, 8 3/4"
$40+

(4) French Ray-o-Lite - Aluminum with Bullseye Lens.
1922, 9 3/4"
$20+

(From Left to Right)
(1) Fulton - "Permissible Electric Flashlight"
Plastic Constructed. 1952, 8 1/2"
$10+

(2) Fulton - "U.S.N." Aluminum with Bullseye Lens.
1935, 7"
$10+

(3) G.T. Price - "Military Flashlight" Plastic Constructed.
1952, 8 1/2"
$10+

(4) G.T. Price - "Military Flashlight" Plastic Constructed.
1948, 8 3/8"
$10+

(From Left to Right)
(1) GITS - Ethocel Plastic Constructed. 1944, 8"
$10+

(2) GITS - Ethocel Plastic Constructed. Has Original Box. 1944, 8"
$20+

(3) GITS - Ethocel Plastic Constructed. 1944, 6 1/2"
$10+

(4) GITS - "Military Issue" Plastic Construction. 1946, 7 1/2"
$15+

(5) GITS - Plastic Construction. 1948, 7 1/2"
$20+

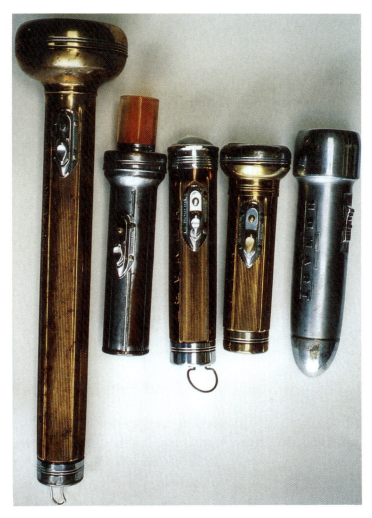

Left to Right:
Homart - Aluminum Constructed. 1930, 14 3/4" – **$35+**

Homart - Aluminum Constructed with Unique Lens Cap, 1930, 8 1/2" – **$15+**

Homart - Aluminum Constructed with Bullseye Lens, 1930, 7 1/2" – **$20+**

Homart - Aluminum Constructed. 1930, 6 3/4" – **$20+**

Homart - Aluminum Constructed, 1939, 8 1/4" – **$10+**

(From Left to Right)
(1) Hipco - Brass Constructed with Bullseye Lens.
1928, 5 3/4"
$30+

(2) Hipco - Fiber Walled with Bullseye Lens.
1929, 6 3/4"
$20+

(3) Hipco - Fiber Walled with Bullseye Lens.
1930, 8 5/8"
$20+

(4) Hipco - Aluminum Constructed.
1948, 6"
$10+

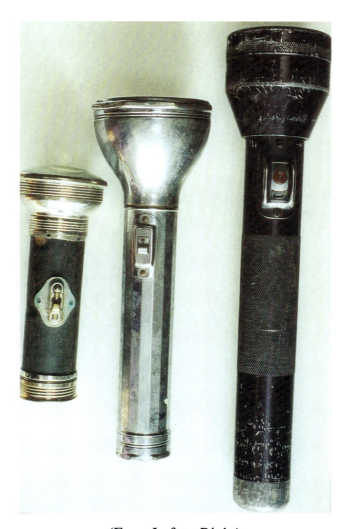

(From Left to Right)
(1) Hylite - Fiber Walled with Bullseye Lens.
1922, 6 1/2"
$10+

(2) Keen Kutter - Aluminum Constructed.
1930, 10"
$40+

(3) Kel-Lite Industries - Steel Constructed.
1955, 14"
$10+

(From Left to Right)
(1) Kwik-Lite - Aluminum Constructed with Bullseye Lens. 1922, 6"
$20

(2) Kwik-Lite - Aluminum Constructed with Bullseye Lens. 1926, 6 1/2"
$20+

(3) Kwik-Lite - Brass Constructed 1932, 14 1/2"
$15+

(4) Kwik-Lite - Plastic Constructed. 1946, 7"
$10+

Kwik-Lite - Rubber Constructed.
(All Flashlights Came in Original Boxes and Displays.)
1961 7"
$70+

(From Left to Right)
(1) Life-Saver Brand - Aluminum Constructed Flashlight with Three Color Bulbs and Bullseye Lens. 1950, 7"
$20+

(2) Lightmaster - Fiber Walled with Bullseye Lens. 1921, 7"
$30+

(3) Lightmaster - Brass Constructed. 1930, 10 1/4"
$30+

(4) Lightmaster "Streamlite" - Brass Constructed. 1930, 7"
$30+

(5) Lightmaster - Aluminum Constructed Flashlight with Focusing Lens Cap. 1958, 6 1/2"
$5+

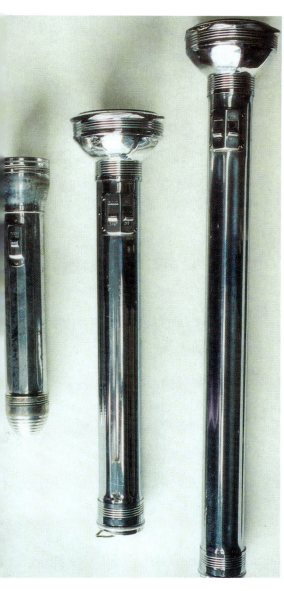

(1) Montgomery Ward. Aluminum Constructed. 1930, 10 1/4"
$10+

(2) Montgomery Ward. Aluminum Constructed. Has Two Way Switch That Goes From Spot to Flood. 1933, 15 1/2"
$10+

(3) Montgomery Ward. Aluminum Constructed. Has Two Way Switch That Goes From Spot to Flood. 1933, 19 1/2" (Advertised as The Worlds Longest Flashlight)
$20+

(From Left to Right)
(1) Niagara Searchlight Co. - Nickel Constructed with Bullseye Lens
1914, 5 1/2"
$45+

(2) Niagara Searchlight Co. - Aluminum Constructed.
1939, 7 1/4"
$20+

(3) Ox Brand - Aluminum Extendable Case with Original Cardboard Box. 1950, 7"
$15+

(4) Ox Brand - Aluminum Extendable Case with Large Head.
1950, 7 1/2"
$25+

(From Top to Bottom)
(1) Rainbow Brand - Aluminum Constructed. Has Three Way Switch That Changes Lens Color From Clear to Red to Green. 1950, 4"
$20+

(2) Ranger - Aluminum Constructed 1948, 10 1/2"
$15+

(3) Ranger - Aluminum Constructed. 1948, 15"
$15+

(4) Ray-O-Vac - Brass Constructed. Has Unique Switch on Collar 1922, 10 1/2"
$25+

(5) Ray-O-Vac - Nickel Constructed. 1930, 10 1/2"
$15+

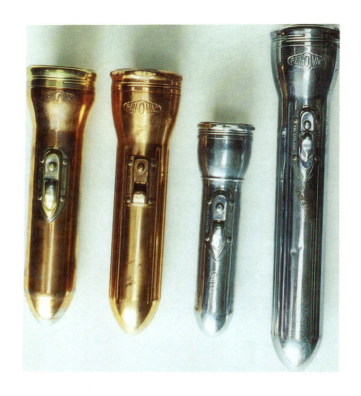

(From Left to Right)
(1) Ray-O-Vac - Copper Constructed, With Brass Switch and End Cap.
1930, 7 1/2"
$20+

(2) Ray-O-Vac - Copper Constructed.
1930, 7 1/2"
$20+

(3) Ray-O-Vac - Nickel Constructed.
1930, 6 1/2"
$15+

(4) Ray-O-Vac - Nickel Constructed.
1930, 10"
$15+

Scout "Sold Only at the Rexall Store" - Fiber Walled With Bullseye Lens And Unusual Switch. 1920, 6 1/2"
$15+

(Left to Right)
Royal Brand - Brass Consructed, 1939, 6 1/2" – **$10+**

Shurlite - Fiber Walled With Bullseye Lens, 1918, 5 1/2" – **$40+**

Sol-Ray - Aluminum Constructed With Bullseye Lens, 1929, 6 1/2" – **$35+**

Sol-Ray - Brass Constructed, 1933, 15" – **$15+**

(Fom Left to Right)
(1) Stewart R Browne - F-90 Safety Flashlight*
Plastic Constructed. 1952, 10 1/4"
$40+

(2) Stewart R Browne - F-81X Saftey Flashlight*
U.S.N. Model. Plastic Constructed. 1948, 8"
$25+

(3) Stewart R Browne - F-81X Safety Flashlight*
U.S.N. Model. Plastic Constructed. 1948, 8"
$25+

(4) Terra Brand - Aluminum Constructed.
1950, 6 1/2"
$10+

(* - Approved For Safety in Methane & Gas Areas)

(From Left to Right)
(1) Treasure Brands - Aluminum Constructed With Focusing Lens Cap. 1950, 5 1/4"
$15+

(2) Usalite - Aluminum Constructed With Bullseye Lens Cap. 1921, 5 1/2"
$25+

(3) Usalite - Aluminum Constructed. 1921, 6 1/2"
$10+

(4) Usalite (U.S.N. Model) - Aluminum Constructed. 1921, 6 1/2"
$15+

(5) Van Camp - Fiber Walled With Bullseye Lens. 1921, 9"
$30+

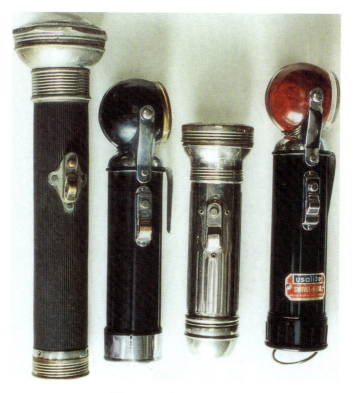

(From Left to Right)

(1) Usalite - Fiber Walled With Bullseye Lens. 1930, 10 1/2"
$20+

(2) Usalite "Swivel Head Design" - Plastic Constructed. 1941, 8"
$10+

(3) Usalite - Aluminum Constructed. 1954, 6 1/2"
$5+

(4) Usalite "Swivel Head Design" - Plastic Constructed. 1956, 8"
$10+

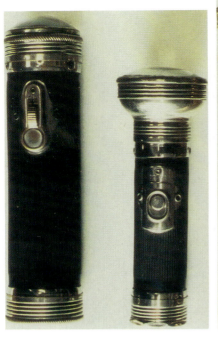

(From Left to Right)
(1) Winchester - Fiber Walled With Bullseye Lens.
1920, 6 1/2"
$50+

(2) Winchester - Fiber Walled With Bullseye Lens.
1920, 6 3/4"
$40+

(3) Winchester - Hammered Brass Constructed.
1923, 7"
$45+

(4) Winchester - Hammered Nickel Constructed.
1923, 7"
$45+

(From Left to Right)
(1) Winchester - Aluminum Constructed.
1926, 10 1/4"
$30+

(2) Winchester - Copper Constructed.
1930, 6"
$45+

(3) Winchester - Brass Coated.
1934, 6 1/2"
$35+

(4) Winchester - Copper Constructed.
1935, 7"
$25+

(From Left to Right)
(1) Winchester - Brass Coated.
1938, 6 1/2"
$25+

(2) Winchester - Copper Constructed.
1940, 6 1/2"
$30+

(3) Winchester - Brass Coated.
1940, 6 3/4"
$35+

(4) Winchester - Aluminum Constructed.
1940, 7"
$25+

(From Left to Right)
(1) Winchester - Aluminum Constructed.
1940, 6 1/2"
$35+

(2) Winchester - Brass Coated.
1940, 6 1/4"
$40+

(3) Winchester - Aluminum Constructed.
1940, 7"
$45+

(4) Winchester - Aluminum Constructed.
1940, 7 1/4"
$40+

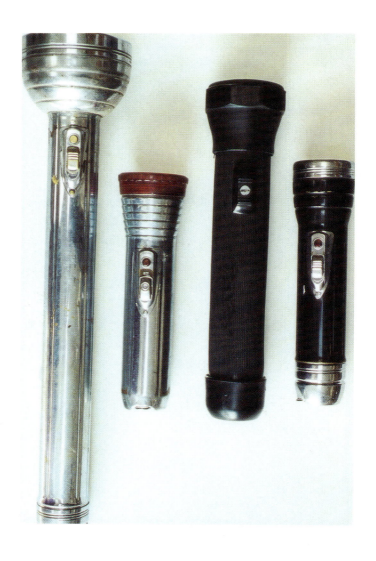

(From Left to Right)
Winchester - Aluminum Constructed, 1942, 15" – **$35+**

Winchester - Aluminum Constructed, 1945, 7" – **$20+**

Winchester - Plastic Constructed, 1946, 10" – **$15+**

Winchester - Aluminum Constructed, 1952, 7 1/4" – **$10+**

Winchester Head Lamp - Aluminum Constructed.
Battery Casing is 8 1/2"
Lens Cap is 2" in Diameter. 1934
$40+

(From Left to Right)
(1) Yale - Fiber Walled with Bullseye Lens.
1928, 9 1/4"
$20+

(2) Yale - Fiber Walled.
1929, 6"
$15+

(3) Yale - Fiber Walled.
1928, 6 1/2"
$15+

Yale "Vest Light" - Fiber Walled With Bullseye Lens.
1925, 4 3/8"
$10+

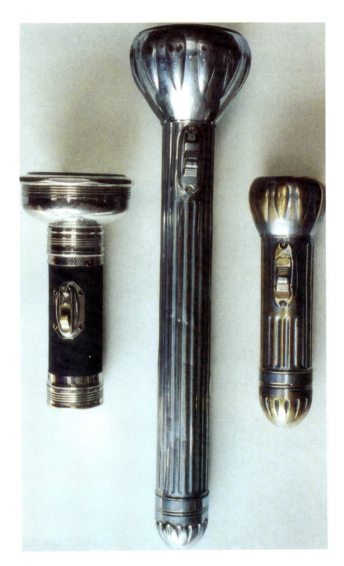

(From Left to Right)
(1) Yale - Fiber Walled. 1933, 7"
$20+

(2) Zephyrlite - Brass Constructed. 1928, 15 1/2"
$10+

(3) Zephyrlite - Brass Constructed. 1928, 8"
$10+

Unknown Brand Names

(From Left to Right)
(1) Fiber Walled Flashlight Has Bullseye Lens
And External Operating Switch.
1912, 6 1/2"
$60+

(2) Nickel Constructed Flashlight Has Bullseye Lens.
1916, 5 3/4"
$45+

(3) Fiber Walled Flashlight Has Bullseye Lens.
1918, 5 1/2"
$45+

(4) Aluminum Constructed Flashlight Has Bullseye Lens.
1920, 5 1/2"
$20+

(From Left to Right)
(1) Fiber Walled Flashlight - 1921, 8"
$20+

(2) Fiber Walled Flashlight - Has Focusing Bullseye Lens.
1923, 7"
$15+

(3) Aluminum Constructed Flashlight.
1925, 6 1/2"
$10+

(4) Brass Constructed Flashlight - Has Bullseye Lens. 1928, 7"
$20+

(5) Aluminum Constructed Flashlight.
1930, 7 1/2"
$6+

(From Left to Right)
(1) Copper Constructed Flashlight.
1938, 10 1/2"
$15+

(2) Fiber Walled Flashlight.
1940, 6 1/2"
$15+

(3) 3-Color Flashlight - (British Empire)
Buttons on Side of Flashlight Changes Lens Cover
From Clear to Red to Green. Aluminum Constructed.
1945, 8"
$10+

(4) Same as #(3) Flashlight Except Manufacturing
Date is 1943.
$10+

Advertising Displays

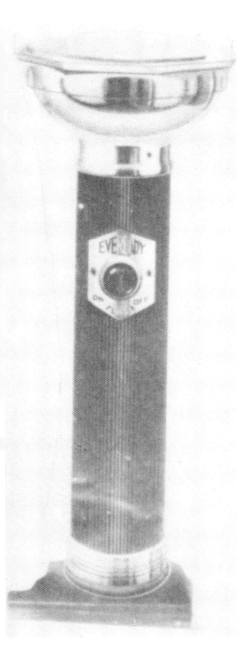

Eveready Flashlight - Die Cut Sign With Angle Mounting Bracket, By The Brilliant Manufacturing Company 1952, 11" x 4"
$150+

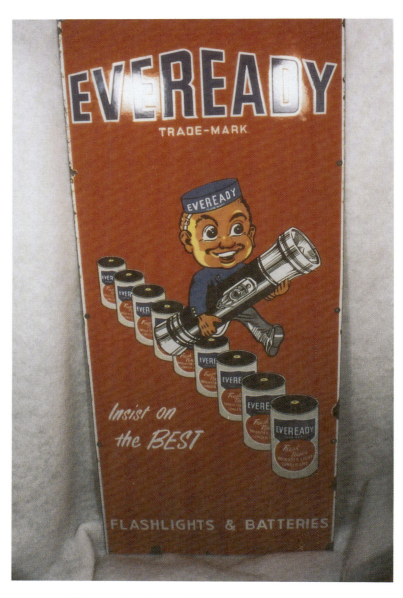

Eveready - Porcelain Advertising Sign
18" x 40"
$175+

Burgess - Uni-Cel NO. 2 Metal Battery Tester. 1924, 2 1/2" x 4 3/4"
$15+

Burgess - Metal Thermometer. 1924, 4 1/2" x 13 3/4"
$50+

Cardboard Display Showing "Lucky Lite" Flashlight And Key Chain Combination. Display - 8 1/4" x 11" Lite - 1 1/8" x 1 5/8" 1930's.
$25+

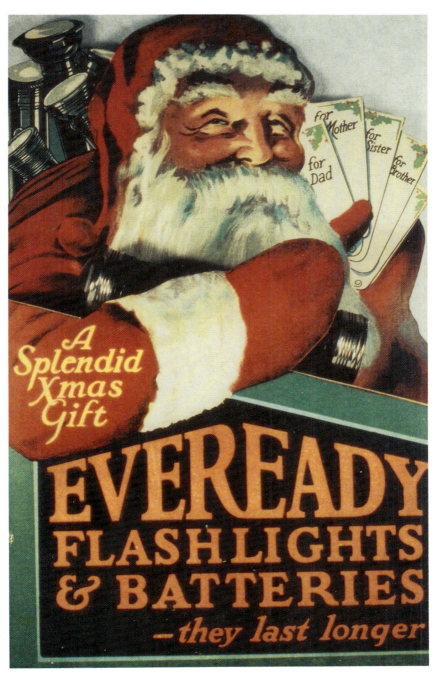

Eveready - Cardboard Display. 10 3/4" x 17 1/2"
$695+

French Battery & Carbon Company.
Ray-o-Lite Cardboard Advertising Sign
1922, 23" x 11"
$100+

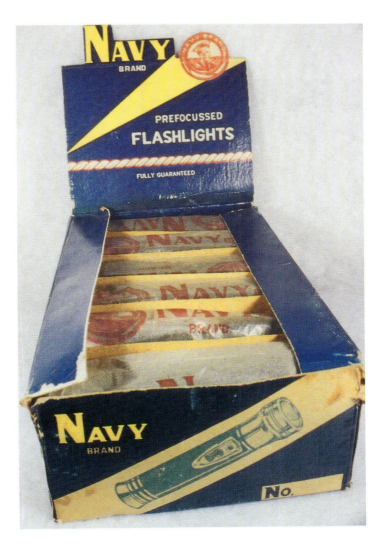

Navy Brand - Flashlights And Display.
$150+

Eveready - Cardboard Display.
9 1/2" x 29" 1950's.
$35+

Eveready & Mazda - Tin Advertising Display.
$135+

Mickey Mouse & Donald Duck
Pocket Flashlights Display.
10 1/4" x 16 1/2"
$495

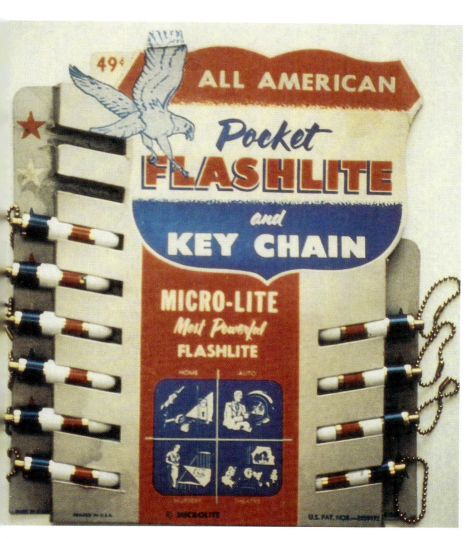

Microlite - "All American" Pocket Flashlite And Key Chain Display.
1937, Display - 9 1/4" x 11 1/2" Flashlites - 2 3/8"
$75+

Character Flashlights

Dog - Key Chain Flashlight. 1950, 3 1/8"
$15+

Train - Key Chain Flashlight. 1950, 3"
$15+

BMG - "One Hand" Key Lite. 1958, 3 5/8"
$5+

Micro-Lite – Bunny Rabbit Flashlight. 1939, 3 3/4"
$15+

Bantam Lite Inc.
Walt Disney's
Zorro Pocket
Flashlight.
1946, 3 1/4"
$10+

Bantam Lite Inc.
Dick Tracy Pocket
Flashlight.
1940, 3 1/4"
$50+

Flippo - Davy
Crockett
Pocket Flash-
light. 1960
3 1/8"
$10+

BMG - Cowboy Flash.
1936, 5 3/4"
$40+

BMG - Red Ryder.
1949, 6 3/4"
$45+

BMG - Cowboy Flash.
1936, 6 5/8"
$25+

Usalite - Tom Corbett Space Cadet Signal Siren. © Rockhill Prod. 1954, 6 3/4"
$60+

Ray-O-Vac - Captain Ray-O-Vac "Leader of Light" 1955, 7 1/2"
$35+

Arliss Co. Inc.
Flasheray - Aud
Signal Gun.
1952, 5" x 7"
$50+

Ideal - Ray Gun
Flashlight. 8"
$20+

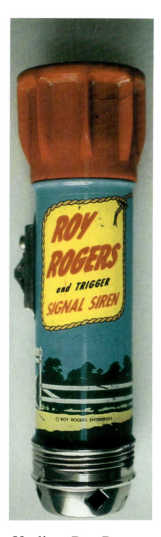

Usalite - Roy Rogers and Trigger, Signal Siren Flashlight.
©Roy Rogers Ent.
1954, 6 3/4"
$75+

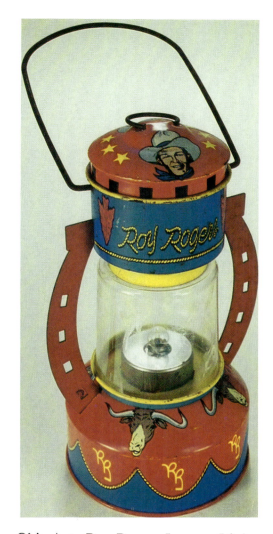

Ohio Art - Roy Rogers Lantern Light.
1956, 8"
$75+

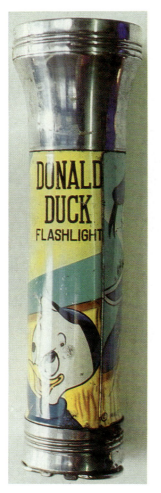

Dan Brechner Co. Donald Duck Flashlight. ©Walt Disney Productions, 1948, 6 1/2". $35+

Aluminum Flashlight has a Buster Brown Advertisement on the end, 1926, 6 1/2". $40+

The end cap to above flashlight

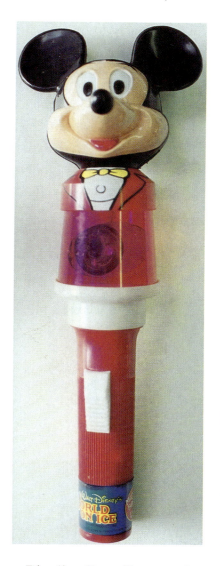

Ringling Bros. Barnum & Bailey Combined Shows Inc.© - Walt Disney's World on Ice, (Mickey's Happy Lite) 1981, 11 1/4"
$15+

Geoffrey - Automatic Flashlight 1989, 6 1/2" x 12"
$10+

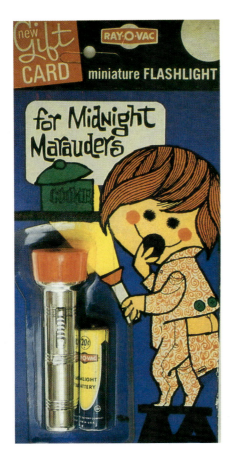

Ray-O-Vac - Miniature Flashlight. "For Midnight Marauders", 1967, 4" x 8 1/8". **$10+**

Pictured below: Jack Armstrong - blue & red flashlights. They have push button switches on the end, 1941, 4 1/2". **$25+**

Ray-O-Vac - Miniature Flashlight. "For Lifes Brighter Moments" 1967, 4" x 8 1/8"
$10+

Ray-O-Vac - Miniature Flashlight. "For Losers" 1967, 4" x 8 1/8"
$10+

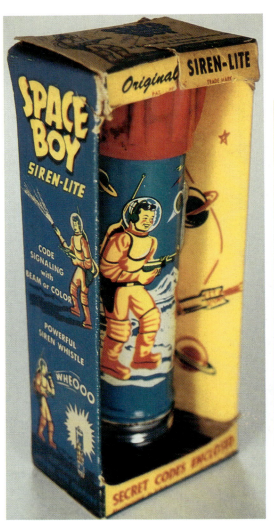

H & H Sales & Manu. Co. - Space Boy Siren - Lite 1954, 7 1/2"
$55+

Ray-O-Vac - Official Space Patrol Pocket Lite, Commander Buzz Corry. Circa. 1950's 12"
$200+

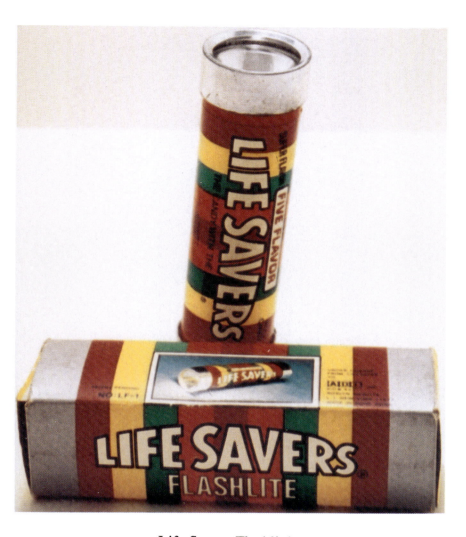

Life Savers Flashlight.
©1980, by ADI Inc. Roslyn Heights NY.
Made in Hong Kong.
7 1/4"
$35+

Rodeo Siren Lite.
Cowboy riding bucking bronco with siren on end.
Metal and Plastic construction.
7 1/4"
$40+

Popeye Figural Flashlight.
Tin & Glass Constructed.
7 1/2" Tall
$115+

Line Mar Toys - Pluto
Flashlight. Tin &
Glass Constructed.
7 1/2" Tall
$125+

Penlights.

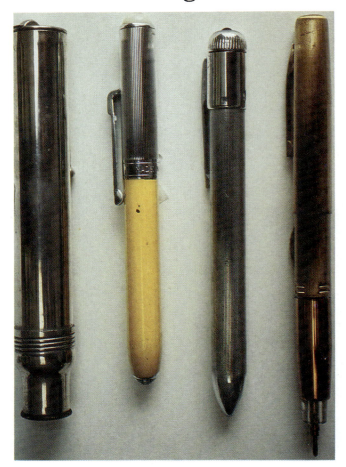

(From Left to Right)
(1) Bright Star - Dentalite. 1930, 5 1/8"
$15+

(2) Eveready - Penlight. 1960, 5"
$10+

(3) Burgess - Penlight. 1961, 5 1/8"
$5+

(4) Unknown Brand - Pen & Light Combo.
1914, 4 1/2"
$10+

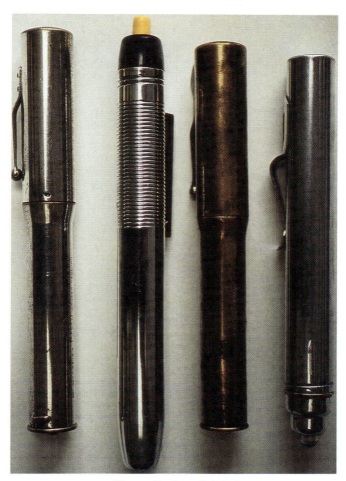

(From Left to Right)
(1) Beacon - "The Ideal Fountainlight"
1914, 5 1/4"
$20+

(2) Eveready - Pen Light. 1960, 6"
$5+

(3) Eveready - Brass Pen Light. 1916, 5 1/8"
$20+

(4) Eveready - Pen Light. 1950, 5 1/4"
$5+

(From Left to Right)
(1) Bond - Penlight. 1960, 4 1/4"
$5

(2) Missile Penlight & Pencil Combo. 1970, 4 3/4"
$5+

(3) General - (Advertising) Penlight. 1945, 5 1/2"
$20+

(4) Unknown Brand - Penlight. 1972, 3"
$7

The Jewelite - Flashlight. 1937, 5"
$9+

Advertising Penlight - Horlicks Malted Milk Corp. 1934, 5 1/2"
$40+

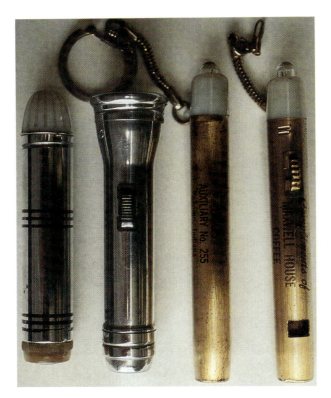

(From Left to Right)
(1) Unknown Brand - Pocket Light. 1952, 3 3/8"
$5+

(2) Hipco - Pocket Light. 1968, 3 3/8"
$5+

(3) Advertising Key Chain, Light & Whistle.
"Eagles Auxiliary No. 255 Kokomo, IN."
1950, 4"
$5+

(4) Advertising Key Chain, Light & Whistle.
"Compliments of Maxwell House Coffee"
1950, 4"
$10+

Novelty Lights

Novo - Pocket Light, 1956, 1 1/2" Sq.
$15+

Allbright - Pocket Light, 1935,
1 5/8" x 2 1/4" – **$25+**

Chrome Pocket Flashlight. 1922, 3 1/2"
$5+

Allbright - Scout's Pocket Flashlight. 1934, 2 3/8"
$5+

Niagara - Brass Flashlight With "B.P.C.E." Emblem 1928, 3 1/4"
$15+

Burgess - Snaplite Flashlight. 1935, 3"
$20+

Burgess - Snaplite Flashlight. 1928, 2 3/4"
$30+

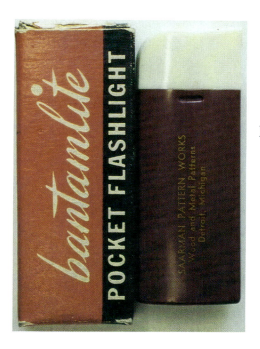

Bantamlite - Pocket Flashlight. Has "Saarman Pattern Works" Advertisement on the side, 1946, 3 1/2".
$10+

Bantamlite - Pocket Flashlight, 1946, 3 1/2".
$10+

Magna - Electric Lighter and Flashlight Combo.
1950, 2" Sq.
$45+

Marbo-Lite - Lighter & Flashlight Combo.
1950, 2 1/2" x 2 1/8"
$40+

Dura-Lux - Lighter & Flashlight Combo.
1950, 1 7/8" x 2 1/2"
$35+

Voltabloc - Flashlight. 1962, 2" x 4"
$10+

Rex - "Ristlite" All Plastic Flashlight
Straps on Your Wrist. 1944, 3 1/4"
$10+

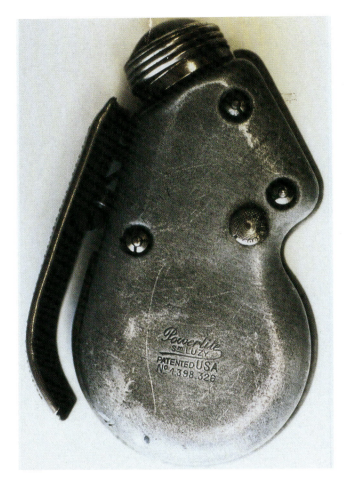

Powerlite "sm Luzy" - Generator Flashlight.
1922, 4 1/2"
$150+

Dayton Acme Co. - "Daco-Lite."
Generator Flashlight.
1940's, 5 1/2"
$40+

Schlitz Beer - Plastic Flashlight. 1968, 10"
$15+

Coca-Cola Bottle - Plastic Flashlight. 1970, 8 1/8"
$20+

Aluminum Gun Flashlight.
1937, 5 3/8"
$30+

Franco - Gun Flashlight. 1908, 3 7/8"
$50+

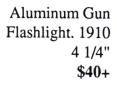

Aluminum Gun Flashlight. 1910
4 1/4"
$40+

(From Left to Right)
(1) German Make - Thin Blade Design Razor Has Small Light By Head.
$75+

(2) Beau Brummel - Thin Blade Design Razor Has Small Light By Head.
$65+

(3) Tedcolite Co. - Thin Blade Design Razor Has Small Light By Head. 1940's
$65+

Lanterns

Grether Mfg. Co. - Lantern.
Model No. 9-S-5311-L
Type No. J-1-S
7 1/2" x 4 3/4" x 10"
$35+

Justrite - "Light-Stick" Flashlight. Model No. 2105-4, 1959, 8 3/4"
$15+

Justrite - Hat Light 1960, 5 1/2"
$20+

Ash Flash - Lantern With Blinker on Top. 1950's 6 3/4"
$15+

Justrite - Flashlight & Hat Light.
1939, 6"
$15+

Delta - "Powerlite" Lantern.
1937, 6 3/4"
$30+

Burgess - Twin-Six Lantern.
1935, 9 1/4"
$25

Delta - Signal Light.
Model No. A2575
1960, 11 1/2" With Handle Up.
$40+

Lewey T. Corp. - "Flash-Aid. 1941, 6"
$35+

Inside View of "Flash-Aid" Showing Medical Supplies.

Niagara Searchlight Company. - Niagara "Cu
No. 21, 1925, 4 1/2"
$15+

Eveready - Dayglo Lantern.
1930, 3 3/4"
$25+

Delta - "Searchette"
Lantern Lite. 1926, 4"
$15+

E.R. Co. Ltd. - Military
Lantern light. 1940, 4 1/2"
$20+

Delta - "Buddy" Flashlight Lantern. 1919, 4"
$25+

Niagara Searchlight Co. Niagara "Junior Guide". 1922, 4"
$15+

3-Color Lantern Light
With Shield, 1936,
4 1/2" – **$15+**

Czechoslovakian -
Lantern Light,
1920, 4"
$15+

Delta - Lantern, 1930, 4"
$20+

Ash Flash - Lantern, 1950, 5"
$15+

Safety-Glo - "Red Ray Lantern"
1963, 3 1/2"
$10+

Delta - "Redbird" Electric Lantern. 1940, 7 3/4"
$30+

Usalite - Lantern, 1959, 9"
$10+

Flashlight Lantern (Make Unknown.), 1961, 8 3/4"
$10+

Richberry Electric Co.
"Super Volcano"
Model No. 275-F
1953, 8"
$20+